D0296495

Exiles from the
American Dream

Exiles from the American Dream

First-Person Accounts
of Our Disenchanted Youth

by

Mary Anne Johnson

and

James Olsen

WALKER AND COMPANY NEW YORK

NORTHWEST MISSOURI STATE
UNIVERSITY LIBRARY
MARYVILLE, MO 64468

Copyright © 1975 by Educreative Systems, Inc.

All rights reserved. No part of this book may
be reproduced or transmitted in any form or by
any means, electronic or mechanical, including
photocopying, recording, or by any information
storage and retrieval system, without permission
in writing from the Publisher.

All the interviews in this book are authentic and
factual in every detail; only the names of the
participants, their home towns and schools they
attended have been changed to preserve their
anonymity.

First publishing in the United States of America
in 1974 by the Walker Publishing Company, Inc.

Published simultaneously in Canada by Fitzhenry
& Whiteside, Limited, Toronto.

ISBN: 0-8027-0445-X

Library of Congress Catalog Card Number: 73-90381

Printed in the United States of America.

Book designed by Stephen O. Saxe

10 9 8 7 6 5 4 3 2 1

301.4315
E96e

Dedicated to
Young People

AUG 28 1991

Acknowledgments

We want to thank all the people who spoke so openly and honestly with us.

We also want to thank: Catherine and Mark Sheehan who sparked our interest; Barys Zajac who provided many valuable suggestions and insights as well as getting the manuscript transcribed and mediating conflicts between the authors; John Griffin, a brilliant editor who reviewed and edited the final manuscript; Patricia Aks, the editor for Walker Publishing Company, who judiciously cut and edited an otherwise unwieldy manuscript; and finally, a lovely, concerned American woman who was interested in the project and so concerned about young people she saw in the East that she smuggled the tapes out of Afghanistan for us.

Contents

A college student, the product of good suburban schools and successful parents. Her goal? To be "hassle free."

An eighteen-year-old doctoral candidate who travels to Afghanistan to smoke hash "in context."

A high school dropout who lives by dealing drugs and goods from India to Spain and back.

Foreword

Almost a year ago, we saw the following headline for an article in the *New York Times*:

Youths Flock to Kabul, Still Drug Sanctuary

The article, written by the *Times* correspondent Bernard Weintraub, described young Americans and Europeans living in Kabul, Afghanistan. These young people were there because living was inexpensive and drugs were readily available. This article aroused our curiosity because we had spent several months interviewing young, affluent suburban Americans for a variety of reasons.

Mary Anne and I have children of our own. She is thirty-one years of age and has two girls, aged nine and eleven. At forty-one, I have three sons, eleven, fourteen, and seventeen. I had been a teacher for more than ten years and had been deeply involved in working with low-income adolescents. For the last seven years, Mary Anne and I have been running a small publishing company that creates educational materials. Our daily work, therefore, has related to the lives of children in a very direct way.

While conversing with our children, their friends, and our younger brothers and sisters, we found we had a great deal in common with their generation because we, too, shared their hope of making a Great Society and the dream of the New Frontier. We believed there should be equal distribution of material wealth; there should be dignity for the poor and the dispossessed; there should be world peace. These dreams were not the exclusive property of the young. Many older people were united with them in a close ideological bond. They believed we could change America.

Then the deaths of Martin Luther King and Robert Kennedy, and the Kent State killings, shattered those dreams. Hope was dissipated for the young and many were left with a feeling of despair. The young people then shifted their concern for society to concern for their personal well-being.

Many young people expressed a commitment to "doing your own thing." They were interested in themselves: their ambitions, their subjective dreams, their internal states of being, their personal desires. They were cynical about the *possibility* of change—"The peace marches didn't stop the war in Vietnam anyway . . ." And they lacked a belief that their lives were directly relevant to improving society either in America or elsewhere.

When we interviewed these people, we were disturbed by their sexual morals and life style. As we sat in their bars or in their homes, we were often appalled by their attitudes. We tried not to be judgmental when a young man of eighteen or nineteen approached a girl of the same age whom he may have never seen before, and asked: "Do you want to fuck?"

Her reply might be a "yes" or a "no," depending on how she felt at that moment. As we pursued the rationale for this behavior, we were told: "It's good to be able to fuck and not to be responsible." Another teen-ager said: "If I feel like it, I feel like it. So I just go ahead with whoever is there." One girl said: "What difference does it make?"

We felt that this behavior reflected sex without feeling or intelligence. These were the youngsters of the affluent bourgeoisie. They lived in the rich suburbs with their own rooms, fresh air, sunshine, friends. They went to the "best" schools. They had plenty of good food and clothing. They were advantaged in so many ways and yet they were following a self-destructive course in life.

Why? Why were so many of them at such loose ends? Why didn't they care more about school, about family, about their future? Alienated is a mild word to describe such behavior. We wanted to feel a close emotional and political identification with the young, but it was difficult to understand an attitude toward life so different from ours.

We realize that not *all* young Americans lived the kind of life depicted in these interviews. However, a large number from privileged white successful America (articulate, aware, generally intelligent, well traveled) seem to be represented here. Normally, this would be the group from whom America would recruit her public servants, doctors, lawyers, managers, businessmen, political leaders. These people traditionally constitute our society's major manpower resource, and will be our future leaders.

We had no answers. Only questions. And so we listened. We asked. Sometimes we commented. But above all, we listened. We listened to find a thread that would somehow make sense to us. And gradually we began to understand.

We began to understand what it really means to grow up privileged in twentieth-century America. We began to understand what it really means to grow up in a homogeneous suburb that functionally negates the urgencies of the larger society. We began to understand what it means to grow up with parents who are preoccupied with income, material goods and satisfactions. We began to understand what it means to grow up without responsibility or challenge, without any sense of contributing to anything outside oneself such as the family or the community. We began to understand what it means for an individual to be given everything he wants exactly when he wants it without having to wait or to work for it.

As we listened and taped we started to see a pattern that made sense to us. We saw the desperation of Malcolm and Paul taking up golf so that they could see their fathers on the weekends. We felt the confusion of Roni who competed with a mother who had kept her shape and looked sixteen. Many of these young people had cried out for something personal in their lives: a human bond. Instead, more often than not, they got a toy, or as they got older, a car.

We heard their repudiation of America: the excess, the depersonalization, the bureaucratization and commercialization, the institutionalized indifference of the schools, corporations, and government, the legitimatized violence against oppressed peoples. But we didn't see them doing anything constructive. Why weren't they hacking out their own lives or confronting the problems of America? Most of them were passive. So we heard statements like:

"Let's turn on."

"I've got some good shit [drugs]. Do you want to try it?"

"Man, I'm wiped out. High as a kite. Flying."

After we saw the *Times* article, we thought that by going to Afghanistan we could find the *reductio ad absurdum* of what we had found in the suburbs. Surely the young expatriates achieved the oblivion so desperately desired by their suburban peers. In short, we thought we would see the end of the line. We hoped that by seeing the exiles *in extremis* we would better grasp where the children of the seventies wanted to be.

But we were wrong. Instead the young people in Afghanistan and in other parts of the Indian subcontinent were relatively "together." Many of them understood why they had left America and they knew what they were seeking. True, they were living lives that their parents might not approve of or even understand. But, contrary to our expectations, they were "making it" in the sense that they were learning about other cultures and histories. They were living with the people and learning about those people.

We did not meet as many dropouts as we had frequently encountered in the United States. So many young people to whom we spoke in the States were not trying to make anything out of their own lives. They had no passion or interest. No real concern. They simply went through the required motions: they went to school, wrote the papers, said hello to their neighbors, showed up once in a while at home. The real fun was getting "stoned" [high on marijuana] or "tripping" [taking acid] with their friends.

The fact that drugs were an integral part of these youngsters' lives was true both in the suburbs and the East. If adults are going to understand what their children are all about, they are going to have to come to terms with a simple fact: just as most middle-aged middle-class adults are alcohol users, so their children are users of both soft and hard drugs. To refuse to deal with this elementary reality is to stick one's head in the sand.

This is not to suggest that we are in favor of drug use. We are simply stating that our direct experience indicates that young people, usually by the time they are in high school, use both hard and soft drugs. There was not one young person to whom we spoke who had not smoked marijuana or taken a psychedelic drug. Further, there was not one young person who had not had sexual intercourse while attending high school. We are not saying that *all* adolescents have sexual intercourse between the ages of thirteen and nineteen. But we are saying that of the young middle-class suburban adolescents we interviewed, all had had experience with both drugs and sex.

We do not ask you to approve of what is in these pages. We ask you to listen. Within each interview we have tried, as much as possible, to eliminate our prejudices. We edited out our questions and organized the material so that it would not be redundant. At the beginning of each interview we have described the person and the place. At the end of most interviews we have stated our opinion. We have included parental interviews as well, because we wanted that point of view represented.

We believe that you will find much material in these pages that is moving. Some people broke down and cried as they recounted episodes from their lives. We all laughed when Kathryn told us that she never planned to marry because she had "a great abhorrence of paperwork." We were appalled when Mr. Klein told us his son referred to him as "Fuck." We were moved to anger when we were told that Mrs. Palmer had published Matt's very personal letter in the society pages of her local newspaper. We were incredulous when Robert described how he had turned on a five-year-old and then taught her how to have sexual intercourse. We know, as you must, that these are *our* children. One way or another, we have reared them. We must take responsibility for who they are.

In conclusion, we are reminded of the old skit done by Mike Nichols and Elaine May. They played the part of a husband and wife who have finally bid their guests goodnight. They close the door, saying:

"Thank God, that's over. I hope that we don't see them again for another year."

"Don't be so hard on them, dear. I know they are unbearable but . . ."

"Unbearable! That's not the word. They are complete bores! Why . . ."

"But darling, I know they are absolutely dreadful people . . ."

"I can't stand them! I don't ever want to see them again. Never again!"

"But darling, that's impossible. After all, they are our children."

All of them are our children.

James Olsen
Mary Anne Johnson
New York City, 1974

Introduction

For years now we have heard about the "culturally dis-
advantaged" or the "deprived": they have all sorts of
"problems"; they need "help"; they are a threat to our
society, because they don't have enough "motivation,"
they have "learning deficits" and eventually they become
the jobless residents of our ghettos—prone to violence,
drugs, alcohol, crime. By implication there are the rest of
us and our children: the advantaged. One would assume
that all or most of the negatives associated with the phenomenon of "cultural disadvantage" are missing in our well-
to-do suburbs, where children are, presumably, well fed,
well clothed, well brought up and educated—first-rate
nursery schools, excellent elementary schools (including
the option of small, private ones) and on and on. Certainly the poor themselves make that assumption; for years I
have heard them dream about life in the suburbs, life as it
is lived in the middle class.

Nor is it for them only a matter of money and work ob-
tained at last. Here is a black youth's notion of what it is

like for others: "When you make a good living and feel you're going to keep making a good living, your mind is at rest. That's the most important thing for me. Here in the city, on these streets, you can't be too careful. You have to watch everyone. There's no telling what will happen next. That's what I learned; and it wasn't at school that I did. I wasn't but a child, when I figured out that you can't trust the next guy, because there are only a few good deals around here, anyway, so a man's got to keep on his toes every minute, every second. Now out there where they have it made, that's a different story. They have a good life. They eat good food. They have good homes—lots of nice furniture, television sets, all the things that make it easy to cook. They own the land they sit on—no lousy landlords and their agents coming around, squeezing out your last few dollars. And clothes—I've always liked clothes, but without money all you can do is look at the hustlers and the pushers and wish you had a tenth of their cash. Then you could really dress up, and you'd feel like a king. And you could have a hi-fi, and fifty records, a hundred records, and if you heard a song on the radio, you'd go down and buy it, and you'd still have money for something else."

No doubt many of us who live rather well find such a view of life "upstairs" or "across the tracks" rather sad. The young man has been taken in by the tawdry consumerism of our society, we think to ourselves, even as we feel suitably "guilty": if only black people like him could get a better deal from our society—and also learn, like us, to be suspicious of its more vulgar blandishments. Yet, who is really immune to the kind of largesse this rich nation offers many of its families? Even among the most refined, the best educated, one finds *accumulation*: books and records; antiques and rugs; lithographs and drawings and paintings; countries seen (and often enough, combed through so that a home might be tastefully furnished); cars and boats and homes and subscriptions to magazines and tickets to concerts and plays; and clothes—maybe not the kind that a black ghetto youth would want for himself or his girl friend, but suits and slacks and jackets and dresses and blouses and skirts and shoes of all kinds and handkerchiefs and jewelry and on and on. In *The Long Loneliness* Dorothy Day comments on how tyrannical possessions can be; they control us more than we realize, even as we keep on looking for more, more, more. At a critical moment in her life she saw the irony many of us may vaguely sense, but spend a lifetime not confronting—that poverty for millions is an awful condition of slavery, while wealth for other millions is no less confining, controlling, determining. To be free of the need to surround oneself with things may be, as Heidegger once put it, "the first step toward oneself."

The "exiles" in this book have their own various ways of echoing what Dorothy Day and Heidegger, two different but equally religious individuals, have found to be true. Throughout this book one meets up with a central irony: born with much, some American men and women have gradually felt themselves to be impoverished, empty, sad— like flotsam and jetsam on the suburban ocean that covers so much of our land. Some have stayed put, struggled privately with their sadness, loneliness, and very important, their sense of shame. Others have been more actively aimless or confused, more energetically willing to say goodbye to this nation—hence their literal as well as figurative exile. And they have gone to a country like Afghanistan, of all places—where no doubt several million men and women, were *they* to be interviewed, might in their own way speak like the black youth I quoted: if only we could have had what those American emigrés had, and for the most part, can still have, when and if they return home! I don't know how the people of Afghanistan (or the reader or I or anyone else) are to make sense of such an irony. The issue is not only philosophical, or in today's expression, "existential"; at stake are millions of hungry, bloated bellies—and alas, from a different quarter, a large number of troubled souls. To draw upon one of the latter, though not the kind who appears in this book: "I feel sorrow for the poor; but I look around at the bourgeoisie in Paris, and I feel the same sorrow." Simone Weil, who wrote those words, was herself an "exile": born of a well-to-do family, she eventually turned her back, philosophically, on much of her secular inheritance, even as she struggled hard not to lose contact with her own roots.

That word "roots," used by her in one of her books (*The Need for Roots*) may be the best one to use in connection with those who reach us through these pages—and tell us how rootless they feel, how deprived of real, sustaining attachment to a family, a place, a set of traditions, a series of beliefs, values, assumptions, aspirations. In a moment of jest the black youth I have called upon once told me a fantasy of his: "Some day, maybe, I'll drown in money and all it can buy." Unfortunately there are those who would only half-smile at such a thought, however earnestly affirmed by someone who has no work and virtually no cash to his name. For the "exiles" of this book the problem is a special kind of survival—spelled out all too precisely and ironically by the struggling ghetto inhabitant. For them there is in that idle daydream a touch of prophecy, a vein of social and cultural analysis, which, in Emily Dickinson's phrase, strike "zero to the bone."

One has to be careful; it is simply not true that the accounts to follow are broadly prototypical. True, they convey quite poignantly and exactly how some of our privileged but despairing (and searching) people feel, and struggle to come to terms with themselves. But there are many who don't at all share either their point of view or, perhaps more importantly, their willingness, in many cases, to live out (in "exile," in protest and self-criticism and self-condemnation) the kind of turmoil they feel inside themselves. Long before our upper middle class became fearful of (and to a degree, deeply involved with) the so-called "drug culture," the confusions and self-pity and brittle resignation of the barroom (and ritzy cocktail lounge) drunk were common knowledge—portrayed in the movies, shown in cartoons, written about in dozens of books, some cheap or uninspiring, some sensitive and compelling. Of course, those drunks (or, to change terms but little else, heavy drinkers, or alcoholics) never threatened us very much; they may have sounded like some of the "exiles" to follow, but they rarely crossed oceans (and cultures) in order to question themselves, look more carefully at what they believed and wanted—or simply in order to live less hypocritically. Maybe they never had to—liquor being legal, and drugs not so.

But I don't get the feeling that for many of these men and women drugs have been the *cause* of their radical disenchantment and estrangement. Rather, they have been cursed by their own inability to make some of the successful "adjustments" others make to the demands of a particular world. Nor do I necessarily say that with prejudice—toward either them or the rest of us. Some of these individuals would be the last ones to proclaim self-righteously their own lives and ideas as standards by which every one else ought live, and be judged. On the other hand, a good number of the social and psychological observations made in this book about middle and upper middle class life possess the clear ring of truth—and surely will make at least a few readers squirm, thereby (one last irony) accomplishing for an exile or two what he or she may have most wanted and felt least hopeful of ever achieving—because again and again one feels in the pages of this book the deep sorrow that goes with an inability to convey to others the depths of one's heart, the extent of one's critical thinking. A little more of this book's spirit of self-scrutiny, put in words that reach across to others, will at the very least not hurt this giant of a troubled, perplexed nation very much.

—Robert Coles, M.D.

1 Roni

"I used to think there had to be something better than this."

After visiting several suburban and college-town bars, we chose The Wishing Well. We felt it was representative of the kind of place young middle-class Americans frequent. Many of the people we met at The Wishing Well and places like it said they went there because it was where their friends were and they could talk. We were constantly amazed at how difficult it was to carry on a conversation. The pitch dark. The blaring acid rock. The flashing strobe. The episodic encounters. None of these were conducive to talking.

Snatches of dialogue:

"How long you been here?"

"What's happening?"

"Feel no pain."

"Check that 'bod'."

"Gettin' any?"

"Want a toke? Got good shit. Meet me out back."

The bar ran the length of the room. Young men lined up two and three deep to get their drinks. The girls sat or stood at tables in the dark corners. In the back room was a small, empty dance floor. There were tables around it. Males sat at some; females at others.

Roni was one of a group of giggling, vivacious girls who walked out of the Ladies Room. The pretty twenty-year-old slung her long blond hair back over her shoulder and sat down at a table, alone.

This place is mellow. They don't hassle you here. Most places around here don't cater to a younger crowd. You can come here and see your friends and listen to music. On the weekends they have bands and things. So it's something to do. A friend of mine tried another place and it was a bummer. We were ''wrecked''—wasted—and there wasn't anyone there under thirty. It was paranoia time. We felt like everyone was watching us. It made us so nervous that we started to laugh hysterically and then of course everyone *was* watching us. We finally stood up very calmly and walked to the door and then started running. Jumped in the car and came here. It was like running home when you're a scared little kid.

If you're a regular you are part of the group and you have special privileges. There is a class system here. If you're a regular, you're admitted on the weekends for free—but everyone else has to pay a dollar and hassle with being carded. A regular just says, ''Hi, Bob,'' to the guy at the door, gets his hand stamped, and then you're in. Also, if there is a line to get in, regulars don't have to wait. This can help impress the hell out of a friend because it shows you're one of the elite. I don't drink that much, but a regular has the privilege of running a tab, so you don't have to pay every time you go to the bar for a drink. And the bartenders recognize you and they know what you drink and they'll serve you first. I guess it's good for them, too, because then you slip them a five every so often.

I guess even nonregulars come here because there is good

music and lots of young people and this place has a good reputation. They are very careful about not letting anyone in under age and while lots of people come in here stoned or tripping or do deals in here, no one actually smokes inside or passes the goods around. So it's relatively clean in that sense and you know when you're in here there won't be a raid or you won't get busted. The guys who run this place are very strict about enforcing a few rules like that.

I guess most areas have a place like this for people my age. I know there's one in Boston that I hang around when I'm up there for school. And it's run pretty similar to this place. Has the same advantages anyway. I mean, the people you meet in these places are part of the group, so it's a good place to get your drugs, too. The prices are reasonable and you know that who-ever is into dealing is not ripping you off. The prices are pretty competitive and if you're like me you don't have to score big to get some dope or acid. I mean, I can get just a few tabs or a nickel bag at a time.

I've known the regulars in this place for a long time. I went to school with them from kindergarten on up. I mean, I was born in this town and so I'm really part of the scene. And there are no secrets between the people here. If somebody has known you since you were five, well, they know if you sucked your thumb or if you're shy or how you do things. Saves a lot of talking. I know that a lot of these kids appear fucked up, but they aren't really. They just don't like any hassles and if you don't get involved in anything, well, then there are no hassles.

I used to think there had to be something better than this. I know my first year of college I really worked at doing things and getting involved. You'll notice in here that there is hardly any mention made of politics or national events. These kids know very little about these subjects. I tried to run with the campus brains and political radicals. I went on a peace march once and got gassed and it was really messy. Did you know that stuff not only makes you cry, but there were a bunch of kids throwing up all over the grass. Good things were happening, I guess. Kids were pulling together to end the war but it's not really over, even yet. And how much did we really have to do with affecting the whole war policy anyway? I did a couple of rally things, too, and signed petitions—but I don't even know what happened to all those things I signed my name to.

So my attitude is like the people here: if it doesn't affect my circle, well then it's not important. As long as other people don't hurt me, well then let them do their own thing. I'm pretty safe in my life. Nothing really can get me. And I'm pretty proud of the fact that I'm one of the few kids from the class of '70 who has made the grade in school. I do take a lot of teasing about it. When I'm in here on school vacation the kids will ask me something like, "Smart lady, tell me why the sky is blue?" But they'll never ask me what am I going to do when I get out of college and that's good. Because I don't know what I'm going to do. In the meantime I'm sort of coasting.

I guess I'm not too close to my parents, but it worked out that they don't hassle me and I try not to hassle them. My mother is a very pretty, southern lady. You remember Melanie in *Gone with the Wind*—well she's sort of like that. And a little empty-headed. But pretty. She's kept herself in shape and my father takes her to a lot of conventions and on business trips. He always is proud of her appearance. He says, "Would you believe my little southern belle has three children and they are all over sixteen? Why she looks sixteen herself." I think that's an exaggeration but she does look good. I used to worry a lot about the competition. When I was sixteen it was a big worry about if I'd ever look as good as she does. I don't worry about it anymore, but I do try to take care of myself and I do the vitamin trip and I do use a cream so I won't get wrinkled and things like that. My father is very rich. He had a very small inheritance but he made most of his money himself and he's not around too much because he's always making more.

The fact that they aren't around too much has led to some interesting parties at my house. Kids are always asking when am I going to have my next eventful party. Usually everyone gets pretty smashed and they do a lot of drugs and since the house has six bedrooms there are lots of places to go off and do your thing.

My parents would never ask me if I sleep around or anything, but when I was a junior and going steady with this guy my mother sent me to the gynecologist and I got the pills. She must have taken care of it with him because he gave me a checkup and then gave me a packet of pills and a prescription and my mother and I never even talked about it. I mean, if I got knocked up and went home that way they would certainly be hassled. They would have to deal with me and the problem and maybe a baby. They never ask about drugs, either. They even offer me a cocktail if I'm home for dinner. There isn't even a hassle about money. They pay for everything and they opened a couple of charge accounts at Boston stores that I can use and they deposit money in a checking account for me every month. And I don't abuse it. I mean, I know a girl who charged stuff on her account that other people wanted to buy and then they paid her a slightly lower price in cash and then she'd pocket the money. Of course she was living with a guy who didn't have bread so I guess she thought she was justified.

I don't know about me and marriage and kids and all that. I'm pretty young yet. As a matter of fact I'm considering going for a Master's in something because this school thing is going pretty well for me and my parents seem satisfied and until I can find a better way to live, this way is the easiest way out for everybody.

Roni was apparently intelligent. As she talked, she looked at the scene around her with a somewhat bemused expression. "What am I doing here?" she asked. But somehow she had never made more than a half-hearted attempt at finding another way to live. Once she had thought there was "something better than this." What happened? By the age of twenty she had given up the search. She had coasted into a life that was hassle-free. Indeed, like most of the people we talked to, one of the problems seemed that she had never been hassled.

There has been no challenge for Roni. No experience to test

her. All her attempts have been half-hearted. And the end result seems to be that never having had to confront or deal with a serious problem, her tolerance for conflict is very low. The suburban scene: good schools, easy living. If you never survived a conflict, you don't know what you can do. There *are* things better than this. There are things worse than this.

We wondered how many people had given up the search or how many were still looking. What were they looking for? We began our own search. A search to find the answers. To find out "where they're at." Where they're going. Where they may end up.

2 Malcolm

". . . I'm a little victim of my own."

As we walked down the streets of Kabul, we wondered how it would be possible to meet the people we had come to interview. At the time, the city was under martial law. We subsequently learned that paid police informers roamed through the jostling crowds. Tanks and soldiers were present and the police seemed to have the authority to interrogate at will, to search at random, and to imprison whomever they chose. The mere presence of a camera or tape recorder was enough to trigger intense suspicion.

As that moment, we looked up and saw the sunny face of Malcolm. Malcolm was a tall, skinny eighteen-year-old, more than six feet tall and gangly. There was a slash of a smile across his face and his owlish eyes peered out behind enormous horn-rimmed glasses. He was dressed in the American youth uniform: faded jeans, a loose baggy tee shirt, and sandals. Slung over his shoulder was a canvas bag with which he never parted.

7

a week ago I started to put my pieces where the other person could just take them directly. It's just an utter lack of concentration. And it was happening game after game after game. I link it all to the hash. My chess game has improved enormously since I got pissed off at myself. But a lot of other things are just getting sloppy. So I guess I will just turn into an utterly lazy slob if I continue to do the hash. Acid is something else. It's almost a religious experience. I accept certain things, you know. Like I believe in mysticism. That's an important thing here in the East. But Western society—I find it hilarious. I often look at it and laugh. Hypocrisy. Power-tripping. Money-grubbing. Power as a corrupting force. My fundamental political belief is anarchism. Which, incidentally, Afghanistan gets pretty close to.

Although I suffer no culture shock, many do. I came overland. You should go back overland. Get yourself on the train. I had a fantastic time on the train from Istanbul to Tehran. It takes about eighty-four hours with just two cars filled with nomads. And, of course, American freaks [often used interchangeably with hippy]. We all come here to choose something. Some choose religion. I look at myself with a lot of respect, and yet I don't think I have any significance. In the infinite, in all space and time, I'm just a dot, you know.

In theory, I live my life within the context of my pleasures. I just want to maximize that. In reality, life is physically painful.

Families are that way, too. In theory, pleasure. In reality, painful. My older brother . . . with him, I've been shat on all my life. I don't resent him anymore though. He's really straight. But, generally, now we do get along together. He's just finished up a Ph.D. in economics, and we talk about math together. But I know more math than he does. I have an older sister. We get along, but she's straight, very straight, a socialite. My younger sister, we get along best. She's just fifteen. And she's not going to be straight. I am close to my father. We have the same sense of humor. We can empathize with each other very well. All of my relationships at home are necessarily superficial, except with my little sister. I resent protection, but I can get along with my mother great. They are all basically so straight. I can't even tell them that I'm doing acid. And you know how important acid is to my life. You can imagine how much it affects my life; and yet I can tell them nothing about it. I give my family very little of myself. I don't know if they sense that or not.

They tried though. They wanted me to get the best education possible. They spent like twenty thousand dollars on my education. It's crazy. And it was boarding school that made me what I am.

Malcolm became agitated. He appeared about to cry. He was wrestling with his inability to either express or to communicate strong emotion. Malcolm's world was a world of idealized, intellectual abstractions that were completely devoid of human content or feeling. As we probed, it became more and more painful. Through his honesty with us, he was gaining some insight into himself. To his credit, he refused to turn away from the confrontation.

It's like why I am in Afghanistan. Oh, it has something to do with mediocrity. I imagine that I will become a professor, that I will publish some papers and some journals. But now I'm in Afghanistan for adventure. To get away from relationships. To take a rest. To go somewhere where I wouldn't see anybody that I knew. That is a good part of it.

Also, I've finished college. I majored in mathematics. I'm here mostly for the adventure. Mostly for the hash. I can smoke hash back home, but I am here to smoke it in context. That's about the reasons I am here. I've got to decide what I am going to do. But this is a helluva place to have to decide. I have no friends. I am responsible to no one. I'm sort of freedom-tripping. Tomorrow I can go to Pakistan or India or I might go to Zurich or Paris. I just don't know, and I really like that feeling.

I had freedom as a kid. My parents weren't heavy; they were light, in fact. I've always been after *maximum* freedom. I avoid commitments. Like I had a girl friend. She wanted to get married. And she would follow me just about anywhere in the world, except Afghanistan. It wasn't the only reason I came here; but it was the catalyst. She started out being very important. We met sometime shortly before one Christmas, and after Christmas, she moved in with me; and then we were an inseparable pair. Everything was just the two of us together. And like this went on maybe until the spring and then I started moving away a bit.

It was simply that I couldn't be with any one person all the time. I didn't want to be suffocated by her. But I loved her in my way. Sex wasn't a heavy element of our relationship. She wasn't terribly good. I've been with more proficient girls. But I was physically faithful to her. Like finally, I didn't want to cause my girl or any girl anger or disappointment; and I didn't want to be the object of anger and disappointment. I finally split. It was time to see if I had any significance. My family asked me whether it was a business or pleasure trip. I told them pleasure, and they knew whatever they thought was irrelevant to me. So they told me to have a good time.

I came on my own bread.

I'm eighteen, and I've finished college. School I hated. I went to a private boarding school, and I was always rebelling. My older brother was at school with me. He was an upperclassman so I had to do such shitty things as call him by his last name and shine his shoes; it was a tradition.

I've been thinking what I will do after the summer. I'm probably going to Cambridge next year, and do more math. In mathematics one can either be great or mediocre. And pure mathematics is an aesthetic thing. It's like becoming an artist. If you like art, then you should be able to sketch well and so forth. And if you want to turn professional artist, it's a big step. You gotta say, well, I am going to make it. And you got to do the same thing with mathematics. But I have to ask that question: can I ever make it? I think I can make it to be a reasonably decent professor and such. But the more important things . . . I'll probably be mediocre. Another reason I came to Afghanistan, or so I told myself . . . I would come here and simply smoke myself out and then go back home and quit. Or else I would come here and smoke myself out and stay. And smoke. I've been sitting on the fence for three years. Constant self-flagellation.

In the meantime I'm a little victim of my own. There are three things I forbid: I have never done speed, and I have never done smack, and I've never used a needle. And since I got to Afghanistan there is a fourth: morphine. I haven't touched anything but hash and grass and acid. It was a trip here. I'm used to tripping with mathematicians. We play chess and discuss math. We pose each other problems and we work out the answers. We play with logic. And it's an incredible trip to get into.

One of the things that I am doing here is observe the culture. I like to check out the Afghani culture, the freak culture, and the junkie culture. Those three sects aren't the whole culture. Those three exist here; that's all. I think what I have said about myself so far has said more than any classification could. Who knows how to come up with one pat word for oneself. If I had to say something, I guess I would say pseudo-freak, because I wouldn't just say freak . . . nor certainly junkie.

Today, I've done eight chillums. It's more than just getting high. It's something like being totally stoned out of your mind. Much more so on acid than hash. Acid is the drug that I find far more interesting. It makes me focus with an incredible intensity. Back home I have three friends who are mathematicians that I do acid with. One was my professor. We're acid-buddies. We would solve amazing problems in three hours on acid.

My philosophy of life has almost entirely come out of acid. I was a philosophy student once, but I found it disgusting . . . you know, the way they pull things out of the air and call them truths. And to this they apply meticulous logic. I tried to tell my girl friend that. She said I seem to have the intelligence but not the emotion. I hated her for that: she always used to say that I intellectualized everything. And she used to come to me very emotional over her problems. And I would try to convince her, for some reason or another, that it wasn't really a problem.

When I am stoned I can abstract. Even with hash. I can

abstract myself from myself. I abstracted myself from my family. They don't know that I do acid. Acid strikes them as the ultimate family disaster. Their son has done acid! You know. There have been some highly amusing incidents around this. I can do acid, for instance, and be at home. And I've played golf with my father while tripping. And did better than he did.

Acid . . . it's where I see all the deity of man. I started with acid just after I turned seventeen. This guy that is a teacher now turned me on to acid. He was a student and I met him playing bridge. And he turned me on to acid. And we got quite heavily into it. We did it about once a week. And then I started doing it about three times a week on my own. It was a lot. It was crazy. But I found it revelatory and dynamic. It was as though I could divorce myself from my body and just use my brain. And go after problems with no feelings. At the same time I do want to help other people, too.

But look at this . . . here. I think that the average American suffers just as much as the average Afghani. Suffering from mental things can be harder than suffering from physical things. Afghanis' lives are simple and they are free to seek a good time. I don't feel sorry, as a whole, for the Afghanis. I think they've got it good.

Can you imagine if all of the children here lived? How would they feed them? I think that half of the children die. The ones that come out of it are pretty strong, but I don't feel that it's a bad thing. I feel that there would be a lot more suffering otherwise.

I considered living here or a place like this . . . I considered switching into agriculture, but I noticed that I'd be decreasing food supply, not increasing it. I might do that yet. I've been trying to pick up a bit of the language since I got here because everything is made so hard since they speak no English.

Is there a price that I pay? I've had a hell of a good time. I don't think I've been seeking security. I've been seeking anti-security. If I had no security to start with I probably wouldn't have been able to take this trip. I've had a really good time.

Afghanistan is a strange place sexually. There is a lot of homosexuality here because this society is sexually repressive. The women are kept closeted and veiled. The manager here has a waiter who is his boyfriend. And they had a fight and the waiter told me he loved me. It doesn't get me off. But I'm looking for a girl . . . a girl who I think I won't hurt. You know, she's got to be a girl who's just the same as me. She likes me and I like her and we get off on one another. But in the future I don't know if I could ever get married or not.

I think I'm good with kids. I had a king-size water bed once and the neighborhood kids liked to come and play on it. I was into reading them books and playing them Johnny Cash records. And they had a good time. We got along. I really like kids. But . . . balls of trouble. I couldn't have them. I'm not going to live my life to procreate. I am other significant things. Sometimes. I dream for example. Fantasies. Like things that I'm doing . . . they're all things that I'd like to do. You know, I dream of myself as a success. I don't like to flash my weaknesses. But, I've played games with people. The sort of ego over ego game. I play them with my very best friends. But I guess the trick is to break through the games ultimately.

Many great people have deeply believed in God. Many great people have deeply believed against God. What I get out of Kafka isn't any great religious vision or anything. It doesn't affirm or disaffirm any beliefs of mine regarding God. It's just a very fascinating outlook on personal reactions.

At this point we discussed a number of Kafka's novels. What Malcolm found most appealing about Kafka was the comic absurdity and the convoluted surrealism of the short stories. We also touched lightly on Nietzsche, and Malcolm showed great enthusiasm for his writings. What was so extraordinary is that every single person we interviewed in Afghanistan had read both Nietzsche and Kafka and regarded these two writers as a kind of milestone in their intellectual development.

I think Nietzsche was a pretty hot thing. A pretty extraordinary mortal. And his superman trip . . . just like what I said about infinite significance . . . I'm saying one's trying to immortalize oneself in his creation of superman and that was one of the, by far, most optimistic lights in his books. Nietzsche's end is such a determinism. And the other men he refers to are determined men; there's superman, there's free spirit. The trick is that you can transcend to some extent your own determinism by understanding more about who you are and not closing off your feelings. I think that's what Freud was all about. Only by understanding the irrational can we begin to understand the rational. But I have a feeling that I am scared shit of the irrational, the emotional, and that the games—the acid games with ego or the chess games or the math games or the acid trip games—that they're, in a sense, all cop-outs.

You may be interested to know that I haven't come close to playing a game, any game with anybody this summer. I play chess with people, but I don't play nonconcrete games with anybody. I've had fair peace sitting here quietly, getting to know new cultures, getting to know new people—not just in a sense that they're different people, but that they're different types of people. I find very interesting national differences.

If I stay here it might be to do something really good and interesting . . . on the other hand, it might be just to sort of dribble away. But I think I've had a really valuable experience. I think that I've had time to do a hell of a lot of objective thinking. And I think that I'll probably wind up doing a little emoting again once I get back to some people. I have to learn to express my emotions at something. And I will. I'd like to have a girl friend . . . not this summer, but after the summer. Be quite happy to settle down with a girl again.

That's the life force asserting itself. The will to live. Hash depersonalizes you in a sense. Yeah. That black junk knocks me into a depersonalized state.

We ran into Malcolm again. He was very intrigued by the book and by what other young people had to say. He often came around to talk to us after we had finished interviewing someone else. He kept telling us how little hash he'd smoked that day; that he was getting plane tickets to leave Afghanistan; that his chess game had improved. He was reaching for a friend. He became extremely loyal to us. When we were arrested, his primary concern was to save the tapes. Save the book.

The more we talked to Malcolm the more we thought how well he had succeeded in terms that would please almost any parent. Here was a young man who completed high school at fifteen, completed college at eighteen and was going to get his doctorate in pure mathematics at Cambridge. Malcolm was the true student, the achiever, goal oriented, academically successful, and yet he had been failed. He had been treated like an intellectual abstraction and thus he saw the world in those terms. But those terms were not satisfactory, as Malcolm well knew. His struggle, then, was to become a full human being and he was contending with that struggle. Alone in Afghanistan.

. . . a little victim of *his* own?

3 Chris

"... an awareness of the cosmos—you just pick up on what's happening around you."

It was a little after midnight as we pulled up in front of our hotel. When we walked across the driveway, someone yelled, "Hi" and climbed out of a VW camper. A young man about twenty-four strode over to us. He had blond hair down to his waist. He wore the ubiquitous blue jeans and a fantastically embroidered loose shirt.

"Hi, you staying in this place? I've seen you around Chicken Street. How is your book going?"

We told him and laughingly asked what he was doing in this "enclave of Western imperialism."

"Trying to get some ice cream. My friends and I have been smoking and we got the hungries. This is the only place in Afghanistan that sells ice cream."

At this moment a girl wearing long skirts and thirty bracelets up

19

her arms came through the polished glass doors. She resembled Janis Joplin.

"Struck out. They said they had no ice cream and then they said the kitchen was closed. I think what they're saying is 'You don't belong here, lady.' "

"Far fucking out. They even hassle you about ice cream."

We walked around the back of the hotel where a poolside barbecue was winding its way down. As we walked to a table we flagged a waiter and told him we wanted some ice cream. He led us to a table. When he suddenly became aware of our guests he told us he would be right back. About twenty minutes later the maitre d' came over and told us there was no ice cream. We asked if the kitchen was still open. He said he would be right back. Another twenty minutes passed and when he returned he told us the kitchen had just closed. We then asked for some drinks. We felt this was relatively safe since everyone around us was still drinking.

"I'll be right back," he said.

While we waited Louise told us about her adventures living in Kabul. She had been kicked out of her illegal residence the night before by the Afghani Army, after she, her friends, and her houseboy had been held for several hours.

Halfway through Chris's interview, the waiter appeared and told us the bar was also closed.

I've been living in Kabul, on and off, for two years. Most of the time in Afghanistan; part of the time in Pakistan. I find living here easy. Easy, without any paranoia pressures or other pressures, smoking hash freely here, and having plenty of leisure. . . . I like the people here a lot, too. Like I couldn't live in Pakistan, you know. Here the society is very similar to Pakistan, but the people are a lot more mellow. You can communicate with them.

It's a lot better here than where I was brought up in Michigan . . . in Grand Rapids . . . in a city. It's healthier here. This is almost like living in the country. The pace is so much slower. I haven't lived in the States in five years. I've been traveling and living in Spain for a couple of years. And I don't relate to anything in the United States. I don't relate to the education I got. There's been no application for it in my life. I still like to follow what's going on there, politically and things like that, but I don't feel involved in it very much. Watergate, and things like that, don't have much reality for me anymore.

I do miss my parents and brothers and sisters though. I am close to them . . . when I am near them. But I haven't been there in a long time. All of my communication is really with my parents. I write them.

I'm planning to go back to Spain in September. I'll resume living there. I've been living in Ibiza since '68. That's really my favorite place. Even more than here because there's an intellectually stimulating community there. I mean there's just so much to do. That's one of the problems living here. You know, my mind is going a little sluggish. The only kind of stimulation I have here is reading. And that's it. In Ibiza I was involved in doing a little art work, doing lumber work. I am not very good at doing that kind of thing, but I enjoyed it and I got better as I did it.

I like it better than junior high and all. I was always getting into trouble in school. I was considered much too popular, too energetic, too interested in noncurricular things. I left school on my sixteenth birthday. It was the earliest I could leave. They wanted me to leave, too. My problems were really two-sided, you know. A lot were mine and a lot were with the system. I always had trouble relating to my teachers. Because, I still feel, they weren't qualified to handle me, to determine a method of increasing my capacity and helping me to learn.

My parents helped me, though. My father has been interested in politics ever since he was young. And he is one of those who tended to become more conservative as he grew older. He's a chemical engineer. Metallurgist. He went to the university during the Depression and at that time he was very interested in archaeology and that type of thing, anthropology, you know. And he finally became an engineer because that was where he could earn a lot of money. A living. He's always encouraged me, ever since I was very young, to read a lot. And I've always had a lot of interest in history and different cultures and things like that. Maybe that was part of my problem in school. A little bit of ego-tripping, too, you know. Sometimes I felt that I knew more than my teachers did. In fact, I *did* know more than some of my teachers. Although less than I thought I did. You know, I'm still really interested in educating myself. I still read a few books a week. But I am glad to be away from school, from Grand Rapids, from the United States.

It was rough for me there. Through my teens and the first year or two after I left school, I was hanging out in pool halls and stuff like that. I was really bored. I had no direction at all. And a lot of parental problems at that time. Things like staying out late, coming home a little bit drunk at four in the morning, and stuff like that.

Then when I was eighteen, I went to California and grew my hair and got into drugs and stuff, and started to get into a living style of my own. Then I went back home for a few months, and that's when I really started my good relationship with my parents. It is really something to be desired. They are not really into what I am doing now. They think it is sort of a waste.

I think that friends probably play a more limited role in the life style than parents will admit, or we will admit ourselves. I think that drugs have taken an unnaturally high place of importance, and are so controversial. I don't think it is that important in life style anymore. I did at one time but not anymore. Like, I think hash is a great thing. But it's not really central to the living style; I think the important thing is learning how to live in communion with nature and the world around you. How to make the best of what you've got without ruining it. Putting back into it what you take out. Also, having good relationships with other people. Trying to find proper male/female roles.

I had a lot of trouble with girls when I was sixteen and seventeen. I was sort of overly aggressive. I was the type of guy that after chasing a girl for a week or two and making her, stood her up and then told all the boys about her. Shit like that. I changed though. Going to California was important for me.

It was '67 when I first went to California. I got turned on fast and for the first time. Before I even got there. Hitchhiking on the way out, in Colorado. Acid at that time was a real important experience for me. And I got very heavily into it for maybe six months. Acid acted as a catalyst in my growing up, I think. It helped me to find a direction for me to take in my life. My first acid trip was like a spiritual experience. See, I've never had a bad trip. I've had rough times in trips, but they were always resolved.

I was brought up with a family that was agnostic at best, atheistic at worst. I was an atheist because I really don't have, or never really had, any religious experiences. And with acid, well . . . I could relate to it as a religious experience. It gave me an awareness of the cosmos and how I was a part of it—how small I was in it, how big I was.

I've had sort of a Marxist attitude toward history. And sometime in my first acid trip, I think I became interested in religion as a part of world culture. Zen Buddhism, Hinduism, you know.

There were a lot of insights really. Like, my final conclusion with acid is you don't experience any more in the eight hours that you are taking acid, but you are more consciously aware of what you are experiencing. I can remember my first trip with a female and the first time I balled on acid. It was just . . . far-out. Like, I think my sexual attitudes were really fucked up until that time. It was really a thing of conquer-the-female and no consciousness of the sexual act as a mutual thing. Sort of getting yourself off by getting your partner off. I wasn't aware of those things and I think acid helped me to become aware of that. Acid, I think, takes hold of you if you take too much of it. And you tend to attribute everything to it. After a while, I just stopped taking acid.

But anyway, after I left California, I went back to Grand Rapids. And I was there for a few months but I couldn't relate to what was going on so I decided to go to Europe. I left by myself and went to London first.

I had made enough money from dealing so I could go. When I came back from the West Coast I brought plenty of acid with me. I left the first time with eight hundred dollars. But even with all that bread, I was like really homesick the first week I was in England. And I was a little withdrawn. I was shy. You know . . . the first time out. I really didn't get off with anyone there and I didn't stay too long. I started to hitch and then took a boat to France. And then I decided to hitchhike to Morocco. And on the way to Morocco I met a couple of other Americans. I hooked up with them. Went through Spain and into Morocco.

And then I split up with them in Tangiers. They went on to the south of Morocco and I stayed by myself. That's when I first really got into hash. At that time I had just smoked grass. I stayed in Tangiers for a few weeks, and I met two German students there. They had a car. And I joined up with them and went to the south of Morocco. To Marrakesh. We went into the mountains east of Marrakesh and we camped there for a little while. I remember that that was really a turning point for me. I think I had been hiding out until then, homesick and all. Really. Sort of missing something and not knowing what.

These couple of weeks, camping out in the Reka Valley, well, they really changed a lot of things for me. I was geared up from the pace, from traveling around the continent, you know. I was uptight, nervous. And this, this just settled me down. And from that point on, I opened up a lot, you know. Up until then, I was having difficulty meeting people. After that, even a place like Kabul where on the surface it's completely alien to what I grew up with, I can feel a part of it. I really feel like I am a member of the human race.

It's easy for me to support myself wherever I am. A little bit of dealing. And I've learned how to make money traveling. It's easy. You can take stuff from here to Delhi. It's a good trip and real easy to make five times your bread. On all kinds of things from walnuts and almonds to razor blades. You buy one place and sell another. Same thing coming back here. Come back here from India with a whole load of Bombay chillums, which cost a nickel or three cents a piece and sell them for a buck here. When

I came out from Spain I brought five cartons of cigarette papers, which sell for a few pesetas each, and sold them for ten afs a-piece, which is six times my money. Traveling you carry these little pouches and you try to carry as much goods as you can. There is a system where you can go from Istanbul to Delhi for nothing. Just on a two-kilo tea [marijuana] investment. I've got it all written down on a notebook at home. I collect this information and I've worked out this thing where you sell like four or six ounces of tea every day at a stop and it pays for your bus fare all the way from India to Istanbul. So like now I can go back to Europe with one hundred dollars extra.

I guess it was in Ibiza that I first got involved in communal living. A farm out in the country. A really, really mellow scene. I learned how to live for the first time. I couldn't fry an egg until that time. I never made my own bed. I just didn't know how to take care of myself. I was a little baby. It wasn't a proper commune. It was just a house with a bunch of people living there. It was a farmhouse in the country. The landlord was a neighbor. His house was maybe a hundred meters away. So we got fresh eggs. Chickens. Basically getting the house together. I'm pretty handy now. There were several different girls in the house. And living there my attitude toward women changed.

When you are living with other people, with close personal contact, you just pick up on what's happening around you. You just learn from being so close to one another. On and off, I've lived there for a couple of years. I've been leasing this house since 1968. I still have a lease on it. And since then my time has been pretty much half here and half there. I want to get involved and get into some sort of export business. I've had my share of financial problems. I've sort of just been getting by really. I clothe myself, I feed myself, I am comfortable. I still have ambitions to stabilize my scene a little. I'd like to have my own place on Ibiza. And I'd like to have something together in order to support myself—something that doesn't conflict with my life style. You see, I like traveling very much and this type of trading. It would fit in real nice. But it's hard work and slow coming together. But it will happen. I'm still working on it.

I feel that work is just a means to an end for me. It's not my life. I like to read a lot, and I like to write. What I'm writing, well, I don't classify as work because I don't do it as a form of work. I do it as a form of self-satisfaction. Whereas money, working to make money, I feel, well, most people I think in the West spend forty hours, fifty hours, of each week doing something that has no relationship to their life style for the rest of that week. They are just doing it for the money. I feel that you should be able to do the least amount of work to make the minimum amount of money necessary to do the things that you are really interested in. If you can earn money doing what you are really interested in, then you are just lucky. This world just doesn't offer those kinds of opportunities for three billion people.

Finally, I decided to come to Afghanistan. I was here with a girl friend, an American girl. I had been living with her in Ibiza, and we came out here together. After about a year in the East, she was very tired of it and she didn't dig it at all. A real flower child. Very sensitive to violence and heavy scenes. And she found living here not nearly as mellow as I did. I guess for a female it isn't. For her it was important to be able to smile openly in the streets without the risk of any sexual advances. And she felt completely shut off from everybody living here. She couldn't approach a male Afghani the way I could. And the females were just cut off. They weren't there. And so her life was a little bit emptier than mine, I guess. She decided to go back to the States. She never came back here.

I really dig living out here, without television. I don't miss that at all. I don't miss Sunday afternoon football games. I enjoy not hearing absurd three-hour arguments about hockey. It seems like every time I see a *Newsweek* or a *Time* magazine it just confirms what I already believe. Like it's just not there for me.

I believe in education. Like in Ibiza I've seen really wonderful things happen. The parents are starting schools for their own children. They are educating their children, teaching them. It's not like getting up in the morning, giving your kid breakfast, and sending him away. And then you go and plug into the computer somewhere. There, parent and child are totally involved in the learning process, with each other.

I feel very strongly about this. The same way I feel very strongly about what is going on in the States. I think it's really sick. And the general population is sick.

I know some people would say I have "copped" out. I simply think I am being honest. I don't know the answers. But I think being honest is a possible answer. Communicating on a personal level is important. In terms of political activism, well, I am a little bit skeptical. I've found from experience that even the worst redneck, under certain circumstances and situations, I can talk to. Any redneck. Me and him alone. But to communicate on the group level, like there is nothing that I could say to the rednecks of America that they will listen to. So, on that level, I just don't see it happening. I think people on all sides, they got their little parties, and they yell in the dark at one another, but it's all one-way communication. No one is really listening. I'm a little cynical, politically. Activities of this sort may be useless. It goes nowhere.

For a time, in '67, in California, I was active. I was involved in a few demonstrations. I think the important one was Stop the Draft Week of October '67. I was maced and clubbed over the head. And, you know, I was very politically naive until that happened. Until I got clubbed and maced, myself. And I saw it happening to other people . . . to girls, to ministers, to journalists. I wasn't active politically after that. It was a turning point, surely. It taught me to fear the Establishment, or at least the Establishment's police force. And I think it taught me that when people assemble in a large group to peacefully demonstrate; it's like a form of suicide. Violently or nonviolently, the Establishment reacts the same.

The thing that went on the longest was the war in Indochina. But has it really stopped? Why believe any dates? They are just dates. If the United States decides to secretly bomb, they will bomb without Americans knowing. It's all bullshit. I think the manipulation is still taking place. Especially at the top. And people still don't know what is really involved. I think the abuses in our society are not something that our forefathers had in mind.

I don't think the vast majority of people are capable of leadership capacities. Like I think if I were to be a leader, I would have to understand what my life is all about. Generally just be together before I could supply that.

I think if you have any real chance for political evolution, then it's got to start at the grassroots. In a sense young people who have become alienated from society can instruct the society that what it is doing isn't good enough and perhaps it can change. We have to get our life styles together. Get a base, you know, a power base from wherever we are. What the fuck difference does it make? I don't believe we should isolate ourselves. Like my talking to people through this book. This sort of thing. It's got a very important role, I think. Maybe I can help to change people. Radicalize them. I was radicalized in my home. Perhaps I am a little bit unique in that way.

I think what most Americans want out of life is basically pretty selfish. And they are willing to get it at the expense of other people. I don't want it at the expense of other people. I really don't. I could never be content living in America. Even a totally Libertarian America, where I would have my material needs taken care of—that's still not good enough. The Vietnamese are paying for it. I don't want that. Traveling has had a lot to do with that. That part of my consciousness. . . . growing. It's one of the reasons that traveling is such an important form of education. In the United States, we are very isolated, very insulated. You don't have a feel for what's *really* happening in the world. Television is real; and people dying is unreal.

By the time we concluded our interview with Chris we were absolutely furious with the hotel. Obviously Louise was right: "You don't belong here, lady." In the eyes of the hotel, we were middle-class respectability. Freaks were people—they were people the hotel wanted no part of.

Chris, however, was not at all upset by what had happened. He seemed to be unflappable. We asked him why. He responded by saying, "Don't hold that guy up. It's not him, you know. It's the people sitting around us. It's like the States all over again. It's like what we've been talking about."

We stood up. We looked at the laughing, well-dressed people around us. Suburbia had been transplanted here.

Louise said: "There's always the old table into the pool routine. Think they'd notice?"

As Chris had said: "You pick up on what's happening around you."

4 Mr. Childe

". . . they're probably defective in some way, just like when you get a brand new car and it's a lemon."

Mr. Childe was a semi-retired executive in his mid-sixties. For most of his professional life he was a vice president of a major American corporation. He had two children—a son in his mid-twenties and a daughter in her early twenties.

His son currently worked as an executive. He was unmarried. Although Mr. Childe and his son lived in the same city, they only saw each other once or twice a year for dinner. He had never been to his son's apartment.

His daughter had been in and out of college, into photography, into para-medical fields, had lived on a commune, and was presently living and traveling with a young man.

Mr. Childe recently divorced after thirty-five years of marriage. After his divorce, he moved from his suburban home to an apartment in the city. He lived alone now.

Let me tell you a story: A boy was in college at the time. The police busted some of the drug-taking sessions in this community and this kid was busted. It was in a suburban community—a wealthy suburban community. His father was an executive. The father stood up for the boy in police court. The result was that the father was transferred by his firm because of the bad publicity. He went to the Midwest—and about three or four years later back to the East Coast. When I saw him again he said, "Well, the wife and I, we put up with just about everything with this kid. When he got to be twenty-one years of age, I became aware of the fact that he was really a full-fledged adult, he was a mean bastard, and that his one aim in life was probably to destroy me when I had done what I stood for." And he said, "The minute he became twenty-one, after having seen him through several sessions with doctors, psychiatrists, social workers, psychologists, and in and out of hospitals, he was still hanging around home, not doing anything. The day he became twenty-one, I rolled up his clothes, opened the front door, and literally kicked his ass right out into the street and said, 'Sue me.' "

I said, "Well, what happened then?" He said, "Well, for the first time, we didn't have an adult male pissing on our living room rug, shitting in his bed in the bedroom, puking all over the bathroom, and carrying on like that." And he said, "I really got the monkey off my back." I said, "Well, what happened to the kid?" "Oh," he said, "he's an arranger with some of these damn rock bands. He's making more money than I am now." But he doesn't see him! No contact. He said, "He's another person, he's adult, we've got no connection. He doesn't want to see me, I don't want to see him." It seems sad but I don't know. That's not necessarily sad.

It's been like that for me, too. I was over forty before my son was born. I could almost have been a grandfather. I always felt that he should learn to stand on his feet, to handle things for himself. I have not subscribed to the boys' club, pal idea—that a father should be a pal to his son—because it would have been completely dishonest of me. But we did do a lot of things

1

together. I think I have been an influence on him. For instance, my son has become one of the authorities on numismatics in the United States. And I got him started in that field. He writes articles and is asked to make speeches on the subject. Most of the discussions that we had at the dinner table as the kids were growing up had very little sentiment in them. We were never a family that went around kissing one another. We are not a close-knit family because the whole family, you see, is blown apart. The boy is on his own. I think he handles himself quite well. His sister, who is sixteen months younger than he is, is on her own . . . and I hope she's handling herself well. I often used to say as she was growing up, "Hell, there's somebody who's going to make some man miserable in this world, by God," because she was sure making me miserable. Although I have a much closer relationship with my daughter than with my son, this may be due to the fact that she and her mother don't get along. That way she turns more to me.

When my kids were growing up, I didn't want them to think that there was any property that I was going to leave to them. I would rather have them understand that education is not knowledge, but it's knowing where to find out, and knowing how to go about it. Always be able to stand on your feet no matter how hard the boat's rocking. And they should develop in any way they wanted. I think I would originally have liked to have seen my son play football, but he was just not interested in athletics. He was not interested in becoming a Boy Scout. He tried Cub Scouting, but he was not interested in that kind of approach. So I went along with where they seemed to be flowing, and tried to give encouragement, tried to interest them in reading, in science . . . they were not interested in science at all. That was a disappointment to me, but maybe they knew better than I did. I insisted that they know how to handle money. I very early set up a system of bookkeeping for the kids. When they could first wield a pencil every cent of money that they received, either as an allowance or as a gift, they recorded as "in," and when they spent it, they recorded it as "out." Before I did this, there was this business of, "Oh, I want money to buy a toy," or "I want money for ice cream," I want this and that. No idea of where the money was coming from or what value they were getting. And so we set up this very strict recording system for money. As a result, when both my kids wanted to go to college, I simply said to them, "How much money do you want for the coming year?" They would tell me. I would write them a check for the whole year and give it to them. And they never once came back for money, neither of them. I think it was due to that early learning of how money moves, and what you can do with it.

But my kids are really very different from me. They have different points of view in music, for instance. See, they were interested in the Beatles up to Janis Joplin, whom I couldn't stand. After hearing Janis Joplin, I suggested that a wire brush, properly rammed, would produce the same sort of screaming. And they looked at me as if I was, you know, an old bastard —which I was! So that was the difference in their approach to music. Another difference was my interest in science, because I was publishing technical, scientific, engineering books. And they wanted none of that. They didn't want to hear about it.

Probably they weren't interested in science because their mother wasn't. I think she had a lot of influence on them because I was always busy working. I was among those who used to say that out of twenty-four hours in a day I actually spent more time in the office with my secretary than I did at home with my wife and children. I was out evenings, too. I belonged to maybe fifteen or twenty different organizations out here . . . so there were evening meetings, and away all day, and doing quite a bit of traveling.

It's not that my children grew up without me; they grew up without part of me. But I'm not sure that they would have wanted that part, or accepted it, even so. Too much difference in age, too much difference in the times in which they lived, the music, the movies, the literature they were reading, their peers.

As I look back now, I don't think our family would have been called a normal one as compared with the younger couples that had children. I think that's true of any children of older couples. There's always quite a gap there.

Of course, I had a lot of pride in the fact that my first child was a son . . . there was a certain fulfillment. I used to say that with two children, we had just replaced ourselves in the world population; we weren't adding to it, neither were we detracting. I was always interested in their accomplishments because it's like seeing anything grow and change. That's interesting to me scientifically. You see them through all the stages of growth, sickness, disappointments . . . and finally you look around, like today, and they're adults, and they're out on their own, and they hardly know you. And they shouldn't, you see. I suppose this stems from the fact that I was away from my home starting when I was fourteen, and just never got back to it. Therefore I don't know about all these things, because when I was about nineteen, my parents had had nothing to say to me about what I did at all. Hell, who was permissive with me? Nobody. And there were a lot of people in the same position that I was in. Why, hell, in my day young kids were sent off to war. No, I would imagine that by the time your children are fifteen, you've done all the damage you can. And after that you should stand by to give advice as a parent.

When I was at U. of Minnesota, you see, one of the brightest students in my fraternity suddenly pulled out and built himself a shack in the woods. He lived there. He was a nonconformist, you see. So it's not unusual . . . I think there are more of them do it today, but there were always people doing that. They just didn't make so much of it—so what!

When I started to work, they had just gotten the eight-hour day. And people used to work forty-eight hours a week. This was the rule. And a week's vacation in the summertime was just beginning in the more enlightened firms. So nine to five was a socialist dream then. I never thought a five-day week would come in this century.

As hard as life was then, it's probably harder on kids today because they don't know what the realities of life are. Everything has been given to them. Everything that's been developed has been made smooth, like plastic, you see . . . a plastic bowl. And you can't get hold of the damn thing. Now if you had to hew the thing out with a chisel yourself, you'd probably be in good shape. Then when you took a hold of it, you could get hold of it. Everything just slides by them. They're left floundering in this plastic age, which is an old term, of course, but there's no roughness, no texture. Everything seems smooth. And that runs through a lot of things, I think. Like schooling. Everybody worries about the dropout. The big question is where do they drop in? Dropping out is nothing!

When I grew up I worked hard because I was stuck with this damn Protestant work ethic. That was what brought you the good life. And I enjoyed it. I did some longshoring in Alaska, I enjoyed it. So did everybody else that I was with. We all yearned to load a ship with cases of salmon so we could get out of there and get back down to the States.

Kids today think differently. They're just making the wheel all over again, that's all. Same mistakes. Like experimenting with drugs. I stuck to alcohol, which was a drug. The only mood-changing drug I ever take is Ex-lax; it changes the mood of my bowels. I take it occasionally.

Before I went to work for a major corporation, I had twenty-three different jobs. But there comes a time when you begin to get hardening of the mental arteries. You begin to get backside spread. And you decide maybe you're going to sit for a while. I don't know as I always enjoyed some of the assets of being an executive. But it was a job to do, and somebody had to do it. I discovered early on that you could become an executive simply by saying either yes or no to every damn question put to you. Saying it right away, and very firmly. And it didn't matter which you said! In the end, you came out as an executive. A lot of people don't want the responsibility of sticking their necks out. Like social dropouts.

I've always seen people who dropped out, I've always seen people who didn't want the nine to five. There have always been people that you'd call hippys today. They used to be out riding railroad trains. But there were lots of them. They were known as "bummers" instead of hippys. I think the big difference is that there's so much more knowledge. There's a greater diversity of things, a greater number of things. So you have to make more choices.

There's a greater variety of sports, for instance. When I grew up, I think there were only eight major league baseball teams. They were all on the East Coast. Well, you didn't have too much trouble following one of those teams. But today they got maybe three or four times as many baseball teams.

Or another example—drugs. There were always drugs available. There were always the Chinese opium dens . . . someone was always getting hauled in for pushing cocaine. I'm talking about in the teens and twenties. You read the local newspapers in those days. You know, they didn't have the organization for distributing this stuff. It wasn't as greatly spread around maybe. But there were people who did a lot of sniffing and drinking in garages and what not. And there was always prohibition, you see. Some people got to like the taste of gasoline, I understand. And bathtub gin.

Or sex. Sex is different today, especially for women. I haven't heard any new sex stories from a man's point of view for a long time. But people are freer today. Like they will live together rather than get married.

I think I was particularly unaware of the fact that when my children were very young, before they could talk even, that they were learning through their feelings. They were often learning things that were quite different from what I thought they were learning. This is due to the English language; it's also due to peculiarities of parents and how the parents were raised themselves. I wasn't in tune with my kids' feelings . . . not as much as I should have been, because I was busy doing something else. I didn't spend all my life, you know, raising kids.

I know a lot of kids complain that their parents weren't with them, that they didn't share their lives with them, and that they gave them things and advantages rather than of themselves. A damn good kick in the ass is what those kids need. I think they're using that as a cop-out. I think they're probably defective in some way, just like you get a brand new car and it's a lemon.

Those complaints kids make are mostly unjustified. They're trying to blame somebody else and should be blaming themselves. I'll tell you, my kids might have been a damn sight sadder if I'd spent more time with them. I just wouldn't have put up with a lot of the stuff that went on.

I've always been the observer, and this shows up in this course I'm taking, you see. It showed up in a strange way last night. Everybody had to close his eyes and mill around in a room. And there was a lot of bumping and so on. And then the teacher said, "Now everybody keep your eyes closed, and gravitate toward the center of the room." Then he said, "Now open your eyes." Now, everyone but myself was pretty close to the center of the room. And I was a-waay off. Now this is the story of my life. I wasn't into that center—but I was observing it.

Gee, if I were sore at somebody, I never took my anger home. I never mentioned what troubles I had in the office. Especially where there were feelings involved. I don't believe in throwing your troubles, especially personal troubles, personal feelings, onto other people. All people care about is your performance, to a great extent. You're kidding yourself if you think any differently. Do you think that feelings promote you in growth and human communication? I'm not sure that's good. It's true that most people worry about themselves too much. That's sort of the animalistic, you see . . . hating, loving. It's important how one performs, but you don't have to get in bed with them! I'm interested in looking at other people as an observer. And maybe recording it. Why this great interest now in the "inner core" of a person? People will start off, you see, by asking about yourself. And inside of x number of seconds I can get it switched right around, and they're telling me about themselves. And that's what they really wanted in the first place. They weren't really interested in the other person. They wanted to talk about themselves.

For myself, I have enough within me to keep me going. Ideas, things to do, interests. I've come to believe that you leave this world just as naked as you came in. And with the passage of a very little bit of time, it is no matter.

When I was confirmed in the church, I thought God was going to give me a real gift of tongues, a real blessing, so I could do what I wanted to do. Well, he didn't come through. I began to be disillusioned. I began to see that the whole organization was providing a living for a group of people who were really basically no different from anybody else. Have you seen this movie *Siddhartha*? Well, the movie is not as good as the novel, but it's a try. And you get down so that the final thing that has any importance, you see, is the voice of the river. It goes on. I think that's partly right. People coming along later. And I think only in a very few instances does someone come along, say, like Shakespeare. There's someone whose works are known, but they know nothing about the man. Mark Twain, when he was asked about it, said, "If I woke up in the morning and looked in the field across the road and saw footsteps a hundred yards long, I'd know somebody pretty big had gone by, but that's all I'd know." There are big people like that, but they're few and far between.

We found it difficult to get Mr. Childe to reveal his feelings. We realized that he had completely rationalized his behavior with respect to his wife and children on a simple ground. He had provided them with certain advantages and opportunities which' they wouldn't have had without him. They lived in a nice house in the suburbs. They had had an excellent education. They had had extensive travel opportunities. Neither his wife nor his children had had to work at a job over the years.

But the idea of a family as a way of sharing feelings was foreign to Mr. Childe. He was like a man painting a house who refuses to get paint on himself, on his clothes, or on anything around him.

show people here. You know, so they'll want to buy it. That's how I earn my bread. I work out of my basement. It only cost me seven hundred dollars to get started, and I'm going great now. I mean, I sold a couple of hundred dollars' worth of stuff. That means it should pay for itself soon. Then it's profits, except what I have to lay out for materials, see? No, I don't have a whole house. I live in my parents' house, man. The basement is mine. I fixed it up and I stay there. It's got its own door and I can come and go and there's no hassles. My parents don't give me much shit, anyway. They're pretty cool people. I mean, when other parents might really freak out, they stay pretty cool. Like when I was busted for pot, a couple of years ago. I mean it was a shock because it wasn't so open then. But my parents stayed pretty cool. They didn't get too uptight. My old man, he really spent a bundle on some hot-shot lawyer to get me off. I got off. Yeah, he makes a lot of money. He's a doctor and all his patients are pretty well off, so . . . Did you see a green Porsche? That's my mother's. I'm driving it tonight. She lets me use it. Or I drive my father's BMW sometimes. Yeah, I have my own, too; it's a Mustang, couple of years old. Sure, I like to drive their cars better. What do you think?

They think this silver trip . . . it's okay. They lent me the money to get started. They'd probably be happier if I had a regular job. You know, nine to five. But man, I told them, like I couldn't handle it. I mean, I've tried working for someone else, but the shit you take . . . and they make the money. I mean you don't, that's for sure. They sit on their butts and you bust your ass for them. Anyway, I told them. Now I don't have to work for anyone, and my time is my own. No clock to punch. I've been doing things on my own for about two years now, I guess. Yeah, different things.

I like to do things with my hands. That's why I like this silver business; I can really work with my hands. Yeah, I could see myself doing this for a while. Sometimes I do something a while and then it gets to be a drag. Or something comes up; like, for a while I was rebuilding these old cars that nobody else would bother with, and I'd sell them at a profit. But it got too much for my parents. Man, one day they just told me: "Get that junkyard out of the driveway!" They just didn't like all that old rusty shit piled up by their house, man. It didn't look too good. So what could I do?

I tried school for a while; it was a drag. I couldn't handle four years of that. No way. I did have a pretty good time. Yeah . . . I partied a lot, got wrecked every night. But I didn't like my classes, and I didn't like to write all those crazy-ass papers. I mean, what do I have to say about some guy's sonnet that he wrote four hundred years ago? I quit after a semester. Dropped out. No, my parents weren't exactly thrilled, I mean my father's a fuckin' doctor. You know how long they go to school! And they're pretty competitive people. But I'm just not into all that shit. People who want that scene can have it. But not me. After that you wind up tied to a job, and one place. And, man, you're stuck. I could never handle that. So, I'm just doing my silver. That's what I do here. Sellin'.

My away time, when I get out of this place, well I usually go up to New Hampshire. I know four, five kids up there. They're going to school there, and they have a house. I spend a lot of time up there. Man, we just spend the whole time out in the woods raging! We all get really fucked up, really wrecked, and we just raise hell. I mean, it's so beautiful up there, all these trees and stuff. And there is nobody there, nobody around. Yeah, we're a bunch of wild men! I really get off on that scene.

I guess I do a fair amount of dope. And I really get off on mescaline when I can get hold of it. And I was into uppers for a while, but I'm not so much any more. I like to drink wine, too. Boone's Farm apple, man, that's my favorite. A few tokes, and some Boone's Farm apple, and I'm off. Sure my parents know. Like I told you, I got busted. They don't hassle me. I mean, they did tell me to be careful, and my father laid some doctor rap on me, but they figure I know what I'm doing, I guess. Shit, I wouldn't be surprised if they smoked some themselves, not that they'd tell me. You know, good example and all that parental shit. Yeah, well, I guess parents have to set some kind of example, I mean to show their kids what they can and can't do.

But man, like so many parents don't even know what's happening. I mean, I'm lucky. My parents are pretty cool, like I said. But some of my friends, man, their parents give them so much shit: "Where are you going. Where have you been. Don't do this. Don't do that. Don't smoke dope, it'll fuck you up. Don't fuck, you'll catch a disease. Don't scratch. Why don't you talk to us?" I mean, the numbers they do. It's fuckin' unbelievable!

Yeah, well, I don't know, like I don't talk to my parents all that much, and they don't talk to me much either, you know. We're into different things. I mean, sometimes we get into raps, but not that much. One time we got into a political rap, you know, a big one. How do you like that? Me! And I don't even care about politics. I mean, I can't fuck up my head thinking about all that shit, and they wouldn't buy any of it. I don't even know how we got into it in the first place, but it wound up, you know, no place. You know how those conversations, "discussions" go. Everybody is sort of talking to themself, and I'm talking to them, but it's really three little—what do you call it—soliloquies. Yeah, like in *Hamlet*. My father's talking about taxes and my mother's talking about welfare and me, I'm talking about how everything's fucked up. It's like we're all saying it to ourselves.

I guess it never was really easy for my parents to talk to me. Like, I remember when my father was giving me *the rap*. You know, the facts of life, which by then I had picked up by myself of course. And was he nervous! My father "the doctor." Well, right then he was my father "the mechanic," because he went into this unbelievable rap. I mean, about male and female parts and this thing plugging into that socket. It was too much, man, and like I couldn't even laugh, because he was trying so hard. I wanted to say, "Look, it's okay, I know all that stuff," but I couldn't, you know? I mean it was a big thing for him to try. And like, at least he tried. I mean most of my friends, their parents tried to pretend that sex just didn't exist. That their kids would never have anything to do with a member of the opposite sex. By which time of course everybody was fucking away.

Boy, I'm really wrecked. No, I don't know what my parents

think, I mean they must be aware that I am no twenty-one-year-old virgin. Maybe they worry, about, I don't know, disease or knocking somebody up, but they never have asked. I think they're too smart. I might tell them! Yeah, I bring girls to my basement, but you know, it's no hassle. Like I said, there's a separate door and we don't get bothered. The basement is like *my* house, you know? I have privacy there.

It's good. I mean . . . marriage? Are you kidding? Not me, man, I'm not getting into that for a long time, if ever. I mean, I like my freedom. I don't want to be tied to one woman. I don't want anything heavy. No, I don't see any girl in particular. I don't want that now. And kids? God, I couldn't handle a kid, that I know! I mean, that's a fuckin' responsibility, you know? I got nothin' against kids. My cousin's little kid, I like him fine. He's great. Like he really turns me on, this little kid. He gets into everything. He's a cute little fucker. But not me! I can't imagine me married, with a kid. That is too much, man. I have enough trouble keeping my head together as it is. I mean, right now.

It's like, there's all this pressure: "What are you *doing*? What are you going to *do*? What are you *plans*?" Like, right now, man, I'm just happy doing my silver, being with my friends, cruising around, getting fucked up. I don't want to have to tell anybody what I'm going to be doing in five, ten, twenty years, because how should I know? Things change so fast. Maybe you'd think you'd be doing this and you'd end up doing that instead, because your head was in another place, or it just didn't work out. Circumstances, you know? I mean, like my father: he went to college, he went to med school, he knew he was going to be a doctor. And like fifteen years ago when we moved here I guess he figured this is where he'd be fifteen years later. Living here with my mother, being a doctor . . . I don't know where I fitted into his plans, what he thought I might be doing.

I think one time he figured I might go to med school, be a doctor, too, but that's just not for me. Like, the sight of blood, man, I just don't like it. And I couldn't take being around sick people all the time, or people who just said they were sick.

Some of the old bitches who come to my father . . . man, they're fucking incredible. They have all these ailments, you know, they're going to die, right? Any minute, they're going to die. So my father talks to them nicely, and he gives them a prescription for some nice tranquilizer, not too strong, you know. And they give him a lot of money.

Me, I'd tell them to shove it, I think. I mean, I couldn't be nice to those people, it would be too hard to pretend. No, I'd be no doctor. Anyway, you don't want to do what your old man does. Because then you'd always have to live with the way he was. I mean you don't want to go around being compared with your father the whole time, all your life. Like, it's hard enough to do your own thing, without having to live up to somebody's expectations about your father. Am I making any sense?

My mother? Oh, I don't know, she's all right. She gallivants around with her friends, goes shopping, drives her Porsche. She's pretty sharp, you know, for her age. She looks real good, she doesn't let herself get fat, keeps a nice figure. Oh, I don't know how my parents feel about each other any more, not really. I mean, how would I know? They have twin beds, so I have no idea if they have sex any more. Like, it's hard for me to imagine, you know? Oh, I'm pretty sure my father has screwed around on my mother a little now and then. I remember one period, a pretty long time ago, when he was always working late and my mom was getting pretty uptight. But never anything heavy; my father wouldn't do that. I mean, I guess it's important to him to stay married to my mother. And I know it's important to her. Yeah, they keep things together. I guess.

Look, man, I've got to be splitting now. There's this chick I've got to go find; she and I were kind of getting it on together earlier and I think I'm going to split to my place with her. Get laid, you know? Yeah, she's real nice, nice hair, nice ass. Yeah, I'm looking forward to getting spent with her, man, so I'd better track her down before she splits.

Twenty-one-year-old Ted really made us consider the prob-

lem of a young man who should establish his own independence. He still lives in his parents' house. And he rationalizes his
need to visit The Wishing Well every night by saying that he sells
his silver there! Ted has yet to grow up and there is little in his
environment to help him to do so. Since Ted lies to himself about
his independence, how can he communicate the truth to anyone
else? Indeed he is only capable of his own soliloquy.

6 Bryan

"It brings on such dreams. . . ."

Bryan was an emaciated twenty-year-old. His face was a contrast between light and dark, soft and hard. He had very long, soft, bushy dark hair and a long pointy, divided beard. His jaundiced skin was tight and shiny with sweat.

I lived with my mother most of my life. My parents were divorced when I was about seven or eight. So I lived a more or less normal life with my mother and sister. I just love her, you know. I try to understand her and she tries to understand me. And she doesn't get in my way . . . doesn't play a real motherly, protective type role.

My mother looks on, you know. She doesn't say I don't think you should go to India. She encourages me to go because I want to go. But she doesn't really approve, I know. I am sure she doesn't know half of what I am doing.

49

Here, you gain as far as the dope scene goes, you gain a whole lot. And as far as the comforts of the West, you lose a whole lot. Older people think if you are going to save up your money to go some place, you should want to go some place nicer than where you are, not some place that they think of as cruddy and awful and dirty. To them, it's like you are getting together the bread to put yourself through a lot more hell. A lot of hassles, and hardships. It's the way they think.

Drugs for me . . . Well, when I came here the drugs were not so big, you know. I came two years ago and then it was really far-out. But my trip this time was mainly to do whatever I want whenever I want to do it . . . well, do whatever I like. And so, that's why I've come. And, you know, I didn't come for the drugs. Not at all. But they're here. And you end up using them, so I guess that's how I got into morphine. Like right now I'm just about forty-eight hours without a shot of morphine. I shot only five months. You know, I'm really lucky that I decided to get out of it when I did. It's been really hard for me though. I've been trying for about two weeks. When I came here I brought a lot of morphine with me because there is a good price for it here. The fact was that I was strong enough to use up what I had put out for myself and still have stuff to sell but not use. But, you know, that's just impossible. When you use it, you get a really heavy flash. It's really easy to see how people get into it. I got into morphine on this trip here . . . taking tablets. You used to be able to get morphine tablets really easily here. And so I started taking them.

I always liked opium . . . opiates, you know, get stoned from the opiates. It's nice. . . . It brings on such dreams. . . .

Things like you don't even think you can come up with. Just far-out things. You drift in and out. You are in an aware state while you are dreaming, do you know what I mean? I mean that you can be dreaming but still conscious and . . . think wow! you know. It's like watching a movie almost. You didn't believe that you could come up with some of these things because you still are aware. And you can realize that this is really going on. What was I talking about?

As Bryan described his opium experiences, he moved his head in a slow circular motion. As he tried to remember his dreams, he slipped into a reverie.

I started taking drugs when I was about fourteen. I took acid the first time. It was such a completely new thing to me at that time. A friend . . . three of us took it. It was about the time that magazines were first starting to do little articles about it, about chromosomes and this new drug, LSD, and they were trying to make it illegal in California, so that's mainly how we got into it. Why, I had never even gotten stoned on smoking a joint or anything. For me, well, I guess the scene then was drinking. And from drinking it was so much nicer. And just so much more clear . . . and you seemed to gain so much more, instead of losing something. I just got into doing that, you know. And I took acid quite often. Sometimes two, three times a week. I remember that we did a lot of acid. It was so . . . so far-out. We just floated away with it that first year. We did large, large doses. A large dose is one good tablet. And we would take maybe fourteen, fifteen doses.

I mean you would have a really long . . . a really heavy part. You know, you build up to a peak and you level out on this peak. It's like a psychedelic stage. Once you get through this rush and you kinda go along a kinda even line that's way up there, and when you take a lot, you know, there's something on everything. And something else on top of that. And still something else on top of that. It's just so strange and different and far-out. . . .

It was really good for a long time. And then I did have a not-so-good one. It was why I stopped tripping.

My bad trip . . . it was just . . . it was nothing more than fear. Fear . . . alone. And I knew it. I could feel it. That was the whole thing. I could feel it. Right in my chest. For some reason I thought I was getting too high. And with acid it's completely in your mind. And wherever you let your mind take you, it goes. If you go out, and your mind says gee, my thumb sure looks big, then your thumb gets a little bigger and then you think, wow, it really is . . . it really does look big. As long as you stay on a good level, everything just continues to get better and nice. But this one time I felt that I was getting stoned and that I didn't have complete control. I came out of it. But I still feel that thing in there, that pain in my chest. . . . A really strong knot which is fear.

We realized that for Bryan we often weren't there. As he reexperienced his past, he was restless and agitated. He often bolted out of his chair and wandered aimlessly. When he rejoined us, he would curl himself into the chair and frenetically scratch his arm. We could see the needle marks.

So I decided to get into some other drugs through my friends. The people that I was taking acid with were smoking dope, too. And I don't even know how I didn't come out smoking it before I did. And it was easier, you can smoke a joint at school. Toke in the parking lot. Or in the bathroom. It was unreal. School. What's school?

Pot's not so high. Acid is more high. Acid is some stone. And that's nice, too. I think that the drugs that people use at the right time are good. They can help you out a little bit. Help you to escape.

In Santa Barbara, California, where I come from, I lived with my mother. She was the only one working. And like she was supporting my whole family—my sister and myself—and paying for somebody to stay with us all day. She's always just kinda scraped along, you know, and she still is now. It's not really low income, not that. Like we always had enough to live, we always looked like we had maybe more than we did. Even now, she is remarried but my stepfather doesn't work, so now she supports him and she works at the same job and earns the same money and supporting him, too. Only now she doesn't have to worry about me and my sister. She was real worried when I got busted.

At that time, I had only been turning on for about eight months. And so I must have been about fourteen. I was in junior high school. And it was like we got found out about. Well, we were pretty lucky. One of the guys I got loaded with . . . it happened that his father was the under-sheriff of Santa Barbara. If we stopped, he said, then nothing would happen. And if we didn't, then his being a high policeman, he would stop us. It was like a warning. Well, I didn't stop. It became a joke. Sort of. Except the punishment I got—I got grounded. Nothing much. It did let it out in the open. I guess my mother finally accepted it after a while that I must still be doing it. But she didn't really know for sure. And then I got arrested when I was seventeen. A policeman pulled us over. He was the epitome of a pig, you know. It was late at night and they jumped out of their car and threw their guns on us and did these maneuvers around us. One guy grabbed me and put me in front of the car. "You goddamn long-hair," they screamed. Fuckers. Country cops. Sheriffs. And they searched my car. And I mean they tore everything out and they found some hash. Then they took us to Juvenile Hall. Well, Juvenile Hall is the place to hold you until your parents come to get you. And my mother came the next day. Two o'clock in the afternoon. Then they have a regular court-type thing later on. And you have to have a lawyer for that. So it cost. And my mother had to take off from work and she had to come with me because I was still a juvenile. The court gave us six months' probation, and I graduated from school a few days later. And then I moved to Colorado.

Colorado was a nice place. I had a job. I was going to be a photographer for a newspaper. I had to send in a form-written letter and check the box saying that I was being good and that I was still working and all. It was real easy.

Life went on normal in Colorado. My life there consisted mainly of working and for four or five months I got up every morning and went to work. And when I was done work, or tired,

I drove home. And then I would cook a meager little meal and go to sleep. Dragged myself out of bed the next morning and went and did it again.

I was still into drugs though. Mainly smoking grass. I eventually quit the job and went back to California. I just got bored, and finally I said I can't do it anymore.

Next thing I know I had a car accident. I used to keep track of the gas mileage. And one time I wasn't looking at the road and I went off the side and I oversteered to come back on and it made the car flip. It completely destroyed it. This was before I went back to California. All that I had saved working went to fix the car. So I got back to California and had no money and had to agree to cut my hair to get a job. My mother's landlord, who really is a good guy, is a lawyer and he got me a job if I would cut my hair. Like he offered me really good money to almost do absolutely nothing. Delivering notices to people. Summonses. I worked for him for about three months and saved up the money to be able to come over here.

When I was working for my lawyer, I enrolled in school. Later I quit, twice. I took mainly art courses and then I quit. I guess the first time I went just long enough to get this loan. They gave me this loan and like I got the loan on a Friday, cashed the check—and like I had a plane ticket to Brussels, and I had to be in school when the check came because they sent the check to the school and I had to pick the check up from the school. And it was getting down to Tuesday, Wednesday, Thursday—and like Saturday I was leaving, you know. My plane was leaving. I had four hundred dollars and if the loan came I would have four hundred dollars more. And it came Thursday, I think, and I cashed it Friday, and Saturday I left. That was mainly the reason I went to school that time, to be perfectly honest. But I didn't feel that I was ripping the check off. I intended to pay it back. I've paid them back a little even. Already.

On my first trip I just wanted to come East. My intentions were to go to India. When I got to Europe and messed around there I was really disappointed. It was still like traveling around in the States, so I was kinda disappointed. And India had always intrigued me. Like I knew it was different. And I had gotten books and magazines about it. Afghanistan, India . . . I wanted to come here. So I did.

I met three English guys on the boat from Rhodes to Turkey. And from there we went up to Izmir and over to Ankara and across all of Turkey and Iran and we got here and had very little money left.

I stayed in Afghanistan about a month. And then turned around and went back. I had twenty-five dollars when I left here. And had just enough to get to Istanbul. And about five dollars extra to hitch to Amsterdam and get a flight home. It was a round-trip ticket. So my first trip out here was really short and I got as far as Kabul. I really enjoyed it. It was such a different thing seeing things that are different. Like people get into acid because it's so different. Such a complete change. You come here and it's the same type of change. I really felt that I was at home, natural. That I was living like two thousand years ago and that I was natural being back there. And so I've always wanted to come back. I didn't think I would be in the States for any length of time because I had brought some hash home from here. . . . I had sent it and I felt for sure that it would be there. And that I would sell the hash and come right back. But then I was there like two years getting the bread together to come back, because the hash never came. But I really wanted to come back here so I worked for it.

I worked by dealing in drugs. And then I got a regular job in Alaska. I moved to Alaska and got into the big, big fishing industry up there. I worked in a storage plant, freezing these big salmon. Alaska was beautiful.

I wasn't into drugs much at this time but I had taken opium. I don't even remember the first time I took opium, but ever since I first took it, I've always liked it. A friend of mine this last time home . . . well, he was working in a pharmacy and he could get these new pills, a pretty heavy pain-killer, an opiate. So we took those. But at this point, I wasn't into morphine because I was still really afraid of needles. Well, when someone overcomes that needle fear, they really go.

In India I happened to have been in a hotel with a junkie. We were good friends and we went together to Delhi. He gave me my first shot and it was . . . the flash is: *pow*! And with the needle that flash really comes out. This is a whole explosion and your whole body itches and it goes hot or something and it does all these things separately but at once and . . . I don't know. Like . . . now, I don't even know what's enjoyable about it. I'm . . . trying . . . very hard to be very much against it.

I mean I am very much against it because I . . . I did it and really liked it and could really do it again easy. But it's such a bad thing, you know. I mean . . . it's something . . . you can't stop. It's really nasty. It's really dangerous. It's so easy. It's really convenient and nice. So smooth. You always feel good. Like here, shooting morphine, you never have diarrhea. Because all opiates stop you right up. And so you're shooting morphine. It was really easy to keep on it. And like I never really realized that I was strung out until I got here. And I tried to quit and I couldn't. Strung out . . . just means addicted. And it was really a flash for me to realize that I was. Because I kept thinking all along that I wasn't. I don't know how I could have fooled myself. I must have known.

There are a lot of junkies in the East. It's incredible. It's why most of the people have to stay in the East . . . because they are so strung out. They have to stay here because they are barely making it. To get their shots.

A habit in India costs about $2.50 a day. And even the heaviest, I mean the heaviest user, he uses at the very most about a gram and a half or two grams a day, so that's $6.00 a day, which would cost hundreds of dollars in the West. So they've got to give it up, but if they've been shooting forever, or over a year, then they just can't stop. It will almost kill you *to stop* . . . the pain would almost kill you. And until there is a reason to stop, or you want to stop, there is nothing wrong with doing it. Like I *want* to stop. I want to go home. That's my reason. Like I can take enough dope with me to shoot up all the way to Istanbul and then fly home; but when I get home I'm gonna have to start shooting heroin because I won't be able to get any morphine.

I am going back to the States to see my girl friend. I've got money at home that I could send for and then stay here. But when you get a letter every week that says I love you, come on home, then I want to go home.

My girl lives with me and I deal dope, so . . . she used to do it and she even got into shooting things for a while. And then . . . I don't know, whatever people go through, I don't know. My girl is not into taking drugs too much.

I don't know if I'll come back here. If I come back here, I'll probably start shooting up again . . . probably. It will be easy again. It's cheap.

I have no idea of what I'll do in the States. I can collect unemployment, so I don't have to worry too much about money. Six months I can collect. I've got money at home as well. Income tax money. About four hundred dollars.

But I'm going back and I'm not taking any stuff with me. I'm not! I'm not! I said I could be taking the stuff with me. I could stay strung out all the way to Istanbul. And have my last shot just before the plane took off and land and not have to go through any withdrawals. I could get some heroin at home. Mainly, I just . . . don't . . . want to. I've decided. In trying to stop I've really turned against it.

Maybe I'll do some other stuff like acid, but *I'm not going to shoot anything*. I hope. You never know, you know. About five percent actually don't ever go back, I hear.

I liked getting stoned. I like not being straight. But I don't like getting stoned by sticking a needle in my arm three times a day. And as soon as I wake up in the morning I have to have a shot. And have to worry about having the next shot and having some for tomorrow. You have to understand that it is really a bad thing and once you realize this, then of course you want to stop. And I hope I can. I'm doing pretty good. As far as smoking dope goes, I just do it. And when I do it, I don't really want to do anything else like getting married, having kids.

Ideologically, I wouldn't want to have kids. With what's coming down all over the place it's pointless. Like my girl friend was pregnant and we had to decide whether to have it or abort it. And, in the end, she had an abortion; but afterward, there was this weird feeling of "Wow, you know, we killed our kid." Should we have done that? I don't know if we could go through the whole abortion thing if she did become pregnant again. Maybe I would feel far-out having a kid, being a father, but it was already too late.

These days, kids are turning on really, really young, almost in elementary school. And it's, you know, open and people know about it. I think too soon. But it all depends on the person.

I liked drugs from the very beginning. I never took speed. I've taken downs to sleep because I find it hard to go to sleep. Yeah. But, you know, I never took stimulants. So, mainly the drugs that I got into were grass and hash. And downs sometimes. Valiums. Sopers. I guess I do take a lot of drugs. I like hash. I guess I smoke a dozen chillums a day here. Could be any number. I don't know. I don't ever count. In India, maybe twenty a day. We smoked a lot of dope in Goa. We would be stoned all day long. When I was in Europe, for a long time there was no dope. So, we were straight completely; but you are always looking for it, you know.

But taking morphine . . . sometimes I thought about dying. I thought a lot about dying when I was shooting up. For some reason, you know. Some nights I would be really stoned. And really flow. And I would think, you know, that I would just nod off and never wake up. That would really scare me. I don't think you would think about dying from smoking twenty chillums. Although it is pure.

I have thought about working—maybe photography again. But you have to really stick to it in order to make it. And that's when I gave up. I realized that I was never going to make it as a famous photographer.

Nothing much has ever appealed to me, except morphine. Starting with my father. I never did get to know him. And all I know of him now is that we just argue a lot. I see him very rarely. Occasionally, I feel like driving up to near San Francisco where he lives and see him. It's ninety miles. And I go. And we sit around. And argue. And so, you know, I don't go anymore.

I guess I just like to travel. I like to see things that I haven't seen before. Like a beautiful sunset over the Indian Ocean. I didn't come here for the drugs alone.

In India, there's just a lot of hassles. The people are constantly at you. And there are too many people. Here, it's really comfortable. When you walk down a street here there's hardly nobody on it. But in India when you walk down a street it's always like rush hour. And it's hot. To buy a train ticket in India is really, really an ordeal. It may take two hours. Most people travel third class and they have just so many cars, but they sell as many tickets as people come to buy tickets. And when the train leaves . . . like it's really a scene. People going through the windows and there aren't even bars on the windows. The train is packed. So you get nice places and you stay there. And then if you have to move, or do something, there's always a hassle involved. So you love it and you hate it both.

But I want to be able to go back to the States and know that I will not get into the shooting again. I've been waiting for people that I was supposed to leave with, who had a car. But this guy is just screwing around. We were supposed to leave yesterday, and we didn't leave yesterday. And then we were supposed to leave today, and we didn't leave today. And it doesn't look like we are going to leave tomorrow, so I just went and spent what money I did have on a bus ticket. Like I really want to get out of here. My visa runs out and I don't want to have to hassle that. For just two or three extra days, you know. So I decided to fuck it and go alone. I have twenty dollars and I can make it to Istanbul on about sixteen dollars for transportation, which leaves me about four dollars for food and so I got to leave now or never.

I feel I should say something that would keep people from using morphine. From using heroin. From getting strung out. Acid, when you take it a lot, you really think that you learn a lot. And that it changes you a lot. And you think: if only you could have people see things the way you see them, then maybe it would be nice to turn them on. It's really sad to see my mother, you know, who goes through life getting up every morning and going to an office. She doesn't like it. She's just a little piece in a big machine and she does her little thing and stays busy all day long and comes home and is pissed off about having to do it. Why not, instead of saying, "Shit, I'm not getting anywhere doing this fucking job," why not just fucking quit it?

But they don't. They go on year after year like that. And maybe if they turned on they'd see that they don't need to do that anymore. You don't need to buy a new car or have a swimming pool in your backyard. That doesn't really matter. That to do what you want to do is what matters. Life is pretty short. And if it takes you all your life to find out that you didn't dig it, then it's really a drag. My main thing is thinking that I want to do what I want to do. Yes, it's selfish. But it's true, you know. Maybe there's a balance in life between how my mother lives and how I live. For me, I always wonder what I am going to do, you know. And it's frightening in a way, because I really don't know. But something always comes along.

I feel a guilt when I say I don't know what I am going to do in the future. But there's no reason to. But then there is, too. I don't know. I just don't know.

Bryan was one of the very few people we met who was shooting morphine. He lived for it.

Bryan had decided to kick his habit and hadn't had a shot in two days. He was worried because he knew it would be so easy for him to purchase some morphine, shoot up, and start again. He said that he wanted to return home to see his girl friend. Did he really?

He was afraid that in the absence of morphine in the United States he would be compelled to use heroin as a substitute. And the expense of maintaining a habit as substantial as his would be too great in the States. On the other hand, he knew that in the East he could buy all the morphine he needed for about $2.50.

We never did find out what Bryan was running from. He spoke of his fear, but he did not tell us what frightened him.

If somebody in Bryan's life had said to him: "Yeah, I know about that knot—I know fear," then he might have seen that he was real. As real as the rest of us. If somebody had noticed him, perhaps he wouldn't have needed to "bring on such dreams. . . ."

7 Tim and Max

TIM: "We have a letter of credit . . . worth about five thousand dollars."

MAX: "Trying to free yourself from your desires."

   Tim and Max lived in an ancient, rented one-room house close to the Old Bazaar. Parked in a narrow alley near their house was their VW van. Both of them wore cut-off jeans. Tim wore a floppy Indian shirt. Max wore a white Fruit of the Loom tee shirt with a sleeveless cotton vest. They appeared very well fed. Max had a substantial pot belly.

TIM: This trip, we are combining a little business with pleasure. We're buying carpets in India, Iran, and Afghanistan, and we're gonna try to get a wholesale business together back in the States. We have a letter of credit . . . worth about five thousand dollars. Like we really enjoy this part of the world. We enjoy India the most, but we are not going to be able to spend as much time as we want.

MAX: We are probably going to go back to the States in mid-November. We have a four-month plane ticket from New York, excursion fare.

TIM: We plan on going to Iran and then India. We want to crisscross Afghanistan. But we will have to get back to the States because I have school. I'm at Boston University. I have completed two and a half years. I've found that taking it slow is much better. For about a year out of the last two I've been trying to make up my mind about what I want to major in.

MAX: Oh, I've only completed about one quarter of any type of college. And since I've graduated from high school, I've been traveling. Was out in California for a while. Lived in Cleveland. Worked to get enough money to come here. We were down in South America a little bit. Here for seven months last year. Here again.

TIM: I had to either work or go to school. And going to school seemed a lot easier. Especially in Cleveland where I grew up. The suburbs. Shaker Heights. And I always enjoy going back to Shaker Heights. It's quiet.

MAX: A nice little suburb, you know. It's well-planned, architecturally.

TIM: I've lived in Boston, you know. So going back to Shaker Heights is pleasant. I liked growing up there. There's not that much that could be wrong about it, I don't think.

MAX: An enjoyable life, you can be sure of that. Easy as anything else. Parents like it there, too. My parents are of the opinion that it's good for their children to travel. My sister is in

Europe now; she's seventeen. Last year, my brother came for a couple of months . . . flew to Spain and made his way to Lebanon, Iran, you know. The relationship is pretty good—not a complete understanding but . . .

TIM: Like there are a lot of things parents would rather not know. Like dope.

MAX: Mine know it but they try to keep it out of their mind, I think.

TIM: It's really something that they can't understand. They grew up at a different period of time where all drugs were heavily looked down upon, you know. It was the lowest part of society that was involved with drugs. For us, well, it just isn't like that. It just happens to be another thing.

MAX: A learning experience.

TIM: It happens to be against the law, but it didn't seriously bother us that it was unlawful. I started smoking when I was about sixteen.

MAX: I was seventeen. Someone introduced me to it somewhere along the line. A friend.

TIM: It's really hard to generalize about drugs. Some parents of our friends get high. And they are like forty-eight . . . fifty-three . . . fifty-nine. And they say smoking marijuana is good. They say it's good for their appetite, it helps their arthritis, things like that. I know people whose parents feel this way, but mine are conservative. Everything they ever heard about drugs was always bad.

MAX: I think the illegality has a lot to do with it.

TIM: It goes a lot further than that. Into things such as

being in your parents' home and dirtying their rug or having dirty ashtrays. These things really bother people, you know. Get them upset.

MAX: LSD is another thing. Like I haven't taken any in three years maybe.

TIM: Yeah, me too. But at one time I was really into it, you know. But you take it and doors are opened and how can you explain it really? The power of the mind.

MAX: Perceptions become much clearer.

TIM: Business is one thing that I haven't been able to get beyond because of the twenty-one years of living in the United States, you know. You get to the point where your parents aren't going to take care of you and they want you to take care of yourself.

MAX: Like where we are at is trying to start a small import business. And trying to realize where that's at, how important that is, and what it means. You could throw your whole life into it and think nothing else and just make money—but that isn't really the way to look at it. We like to do it because it's enjoyable—we like working at these things, rugs, and we enjoy being able to travel and making it pay for itself. I plan on taking a course in Hindi.

TIM: If it was purely business we probably wouldn't be doing it. Like dealing with these people . . . it's pretty aggravating. It's just a different type of mind, really. The systems of bureaucracy that they have are aggravating. You can deal with it, but it certainly isn't pleasurable.

MAX: We've been here about three weeks now. Our first week here was taken up with our buying. Our second week was taken up with finding a vehicle, and getting our packages ready for shipment and sending them. Taking them to customs took like three days.

TIM: And business bribery is tied into this culture . . . almost a way of living. The people get paid so poorly that they are willing to take a baksheesh [bribe]. But everything gets relative. This aggravation's not like prison.

I was in prison for nine and a half months. For dope. After I first got out of school. And like it wasn't particularly heavy or anything like you read in magazines. But there were points when it was a pretty strong atmosphere. You learn a lot from that, too, I think. You learn to live confined with eight people or thirteen people in a cell, and not getting uptight or fighting constantly. It was traumatic, yes. But, you see, like inside . . . well, it was interesting for the look it gave me of the American judicial system. I mean there was a lot of bullshit being thrown around. You knew you were going to end up making a deal of some type. If you went to court, you were going to get screwed; you knew that. Because it was in Orange County, California, which is a pretty conservative place. And it was a fairly large drug bust. If you pick out twelve average citizens off the street, and you call them in there for a trial, and there is some young kid sitting there that just got arrested with seventy pounds of marijuana, you know . . . no way they are not going to send him to prison. So all the time it was what kind of a deal are you going to make. And it was like holding out. Like the person that I got busted with got bailed out. But if we had both been bailed out we would have been in a much better dealing position. After four months of sitting in a cell you were ready to take anything that sounded good. I couldn't get bailed out because of some strange things. My parents really didn't know how to react to the whole situation. At first, the bail started off as $22,000, which nobody had. But then it got down to $9,600, which they could have gotten together but wouldn't pay.

MAX: Some of the guys raised the money and we sent it to them.

TIM: Yes. But the lawyer told my parents that if I got out of jail that I would leave the country. Then this lawyer that I had paid $5,000 for, he tells them that if I get out of jail that I'm going to get shot because with this amount of dope it was obviously some kind of Mafia-type thing and they were going to get back at me. It was just two nineteen-year-old kids buying some marijuana. It probably happens a hundred times a day all over the United States.

MAX: You see, Tim and I started dealing when we were in high school. And this was a big deal for a group of us. He was supposed to get it to us and we were going to split it up and deal it locally. After my first year in high school, I never asked my parents for money. I dealt. I accumulated this money from dealing until I reached the point where we were going to start a legal business. That pot cost us $12,700. The seventy pounds. This happened like three years ago.

TIM: The price of drugs was a little different then. After high school I made about $3,200. Like I didn't feel that I was dealing that much, but I guess I was. But that paid for going out to California. I went out there and got a nice place, outside of Oakland. Was living comfortable. And doing a few things. But after I got busted, I came back to Ohio and went to school . . . mostly didn't do anything. Went down to South America. When I got home from jail, my parents never really said, "I told you so." They just kinda let it go. And they rationalized not giving bail. They didn't have the money and they would have had to take a loan and this and that. And it was impossible to get it together. And like now I was already out, so I wasn't prepared to argue with them. In jail, I was only allowed three-minute phone calls and trying to argue with them to put up a bond and, you know, in three minutes or five minutes—it was pretty hard when your mother is crying and your sister is crying and your father is shaking his head. But I think I should have been bailed out.

MAX: And then he could have beaten the rap.

TIM: Right. Now that I've been through the situation, I know that if you got the money, you can beat anything.

When I got arrested, I also had 1,000 tabs of mescaline. But these never turned up; I don't know where they went. But, you know, like I wasn't about to ask anybody where they were. I never trusted my lawyer. He'd go into his office in his tennis suit. Just too busy a man to bother with me.

But I learned; I don't deal at all anymore. Right. I figure you got so many chances to do things and, you know, like I went to jail once, and if I went again, it would be for a good long time. The money just isn't that important to me. Most of that money I kept hidden in books and stuff in my room. I couldn't think of things to spend it on. I put on maybe twenty-five pounds eating all this garbage. You don't have anything to do, so you go out and eat.

Like another thing: Well, I've always been interested in art. My father is an artist. I can't draw well or anything, but I have a lot of art that I own and a lot of antiques and things—but mostly, I get them through trading or through people that my parents know . . . by trading them paintings or whatever. I don't even really like to spend money on that type of thing. If a potter creates a nice set of dishes, I'd much rather give him a painting in exchange for the pottery than to give some money. That way, I feel it's more of an equal exchange. Also there's no obligation—which is one reason we didn't bring our old ladies with us. It is hard to travel with an old lady, but that isn't the reason we don't have one. To be able to really get a good old lady together, I would think you would have to be somewhat stable, you know. It's hard hitting this. I haven't been any place for longer than nine months. But it's conceivable to me that by the time I am ready to get married—I'm twenty-two now —marriage might be good for me in the late twenties or early thirties. By that time marriage might be a more important thing than just living with somebody.

MAX: I don't know exactly what that kind of scene means. To me, the ideal thing would be to live with a small group of very close friends. Very close friends. My friends mean as much to me as my parents, maybe even more.

TIM: But many attitudes have been shaped by my parents.

MAX: We see ourselves as trying to substantiate our future with buying some land somewhere. It's a good possibility that it will be in the States. It's so much easier to get things together where you've been brought up.

TIM: The experience of living can be fuller than staying in one community. I think you might have a tendency to stagnate in a small town. Like in prison it's amazing how fast time passes because you are in such a routine. Every day was so similar that it became impossible to separate them. And I think this happens as well living in a community, working, a nine-to-five job every day. You become stagnant and you tend not to think. You go home and have a few beers, watch TV. Maybe you get high. Then you go to sleep. You wake up the next morning and do the same thing. You take two weeks off in the summer for a vacation, get a week at Christmas, and the year passes. And then the years pass. And then you retire and . . . Of course, there is more to it than that.

MAX: The way I look at it, what it comes down to is people fitting into things just for the basic need of money to survive. Instead of fitting into things because they like to do the things, you know.

TIM: I kinda feel that regardless of who you are or what you are you owe a social debt. I always try to keep it in mind. But what can you do about it, really? Especially here. You think about it. You see a beggar and you know that you've already given to ten beggars that day and you see another one and you feel sorry for him, but you can't give it again. What can you do? It's the same in the States. You feel bad about people living in the ghetto. . . .

Like, for example, one time I was working in a factory. There was this guy that I was friendly with, a black guy, and he had dropped out of school . . . probably when he was in ninth or tenth grade. Not real bright. Seemed like his reading ability wasn't good. When we read the newspaper at lunch, it would seem that he would have a little bit of difficulty. And he went to take a driver's test, you know, twenty-five years old, and this was for the probationary test, just the written test. There are twenty questions and he flunked it. A driver's test just isn't that difficult. "What does this sign mean? What do you do when you turn right?" And like you feel sorry for him and you know that it's happened to thousands and millions of other people. But what can you really do? When he flunked it and he told me, "It was no big deal. Just a little tougher than I thought." But if I had said, "Hey, let me help you, let me show you what to do," he would have thought, "Are you kidding me? Do you think I am some kind of moron?" It would have been possibly more insulting to him to try to offer him some type of help. I think it's gotten to a point where changing people's lives and changing institutions are such major jobs that it would take more than a few lifetimes.

MAX: In Afghanistan you begin to wonder about things like codes of ethics. You develop a code of ethics, partly brought on by religion—by religious instruction at an early age. Like that you shouldn't masturbate or something. And then you find out by the time you're twenty that it's a bunch of shit.

TIM: Here, the code of ethics is different. You figure being a beggar here isn't a bad thing. But if you were a beggar in the streets of New York, things would be a lot rougher. . . . The poor people here are in better condition than the people in the States because they don't know. If you have a television, then you can know for sure that you are a poor person. And you might start drinking a lot, so you don't give a goddamn. But here, the people don't know. Possibly they are better off.

MAX: There are all different places in society and they just happen to rest at the bottom. In America, it's always: strive for the top. In India, it's much different. If you are a beggar, then you're a beggar. Obviously you can't help it because that's the way your reincarnation came about. People accept that. But that's not the way in the States. It's hard reconciling the differences. It's impossible. You have to set up a mental defense against it. What can you do? Take everything out of your pockets and put it on the ground?

The black person has definitely been uplifted in the last twenty years. Coming from a pretty well-to-do suburb like Shaker Heights, you see a really large number of black people coming in, driving nice cars, having nice houses, raising nice suburban families. Ten years ago, you wouldn't have dreamed of seeing this.

TIM: You see we're really young and you can hardly say that our life has come to a point where we know all the answers. So many of our years were spent in school and involved in certain other things that kept us pretty much in a set pattern. In the last three years we've been able to discover ourselves. Who can tell how our lives will turn out? You can see the changes that have come about in the last ten years since the sixties . . . where people first started taking drugs and this whole type of thing. I think it's been a really good thing. I think it's had one of the largest impacts on American society ever . . . even European society.

MAX: It's opened a new consciousness-type thing.

TIM: Look at some of the things that are going on now in the States. Like Krishnas on the streets. People getting high. It's worked out fairly well. For myself, I just try to act toward someone else with as pure a heart as possible. And I know perfectly well that I can be much purer than I am. I am carrying around a lot of money, doing a very nice trip. But at this point I haven't been able to reconcile the fact that I am in this position of some money and maybe some day I won't be. I would like to reconcile that fact.

MAX: If everybody just did the little bit that they could do. Maybe it isn't much. Just being friendly. Establishing a good relationship with an Afghani, or some other nationality, or people with long hair. Maybe that little bit of good will change something. Many people are afraid of changes that they don't understand. And then you tend to alienate or polarize those people by taking too drastic an action.

TIM: Yeah. By my being the first person working in the factory with long hair, by just being a nice cooperative person, not hassling them, they didn't get down on my trip. I didn't get down on theirs. We got along real well. We both learned something. And like all of a sudden they began to wonder why they had never hired somebody with long hair before.

Tim and Max are American businessmen. They are dealing for goods they can sell back home. They are a little different, true; but how much so? They reject the Establishment, but not money-making. Here are two young men who seemingly embody American values: religious moral training, profit orientation, desire for success.

They are not here; they're there. Why?

8 Paul

"I mean, no obligations. They can take care of themselves."

Paul was a neat, well-dressed twenty-three-year-old with shorter hair than most. Even his jeans looked pressed.

"Can't wear my hair as long as I'd like. I mean, I'm doing the commuter train scene these days."

Paul was standing at the back of The Wishing Well. He was directly across from the door of the Ladies Room. As the girls would go in and out, he'd give them a big "Hi," call them by name.

"Check that cute ass."

Well, I've been in and out of a few schools. Graduated from high school in '69. That was fun. I mean, we did a lot of good stuff in high school. Not too much trouble. Anything we did, almost, was written off to our "just being boys." You know you're almost expected to goof a little. Otherwise you're not normal. Back then this was a really straight town. Prided itself on having no drugs. Everyone drank, but what's drinking, expecially with guys around here. I mean like you're either a jock or a party boy or your old man is a nervous wreck that there's something wrong with you. Then you're supposed to get your shit together, go off to college and become a professional. Professional anything but a party boy.

Then in the summer of '69, right after graduation, drugs really did this town. I mean before that there were a couple of people that smoked a little marijuana, but no real potheads or anything. Then that summer all our friends came back from the great American campuses with the new youth trip. Pot came to the suburbs packed in everybody's school trunk. It must have been the first time that everybody unpacked their own trunks. Could you see all these mothers unpacking funny weeds? Anyway, this place was a hangout and all of a sudden everybody was here dealing. We all went to hell that summer. July was pot and then we moved right into bigger stuff in August. Hell, that summer there was acid and mesc and cocaine and even peyote buttons. Everybody always had the best shit and you went and did it. And it *was* better than the shit you had.

Well, after this really great summer I packed myself off to college in Denver. Actually I tooled out there in this seven-thousand-dollar graduation present. Spent a lot of time skiing and really getting into drugs. Ran into a little cash problem so I ended up selling the car. Boy, did that piss my old man. Communication dropped to a low point after what he still calls "the sale." When I came home that spring I was a little wasted and had not been invited back for the next year. Spent that summer being hounded by my old man and making late applications for school. It was either find a new place to go or go to work at my old man's place. He is president of a food coloring company. He said I should follow my own career or go to work for him so I could learn the ropes. I ended up in a mid-west school, in the boondocks. I was trying to bring my grades up so I could transfer to a better school. That scene really sucked, so I dropped out. But I had been accepted at the University of

Vermont for the next fall. I told my old man and that kind of cooled him down a little.

I just hung around then. I considered myself on vacation till the following fall. I vacationed in California with a couple of guys from here. I was not the only one having trouble finding himself, so we all vacationed and partied to California and back. It was great out there. One of the guy's sisters had a pad in Santa Barbara and so we crashed there for a while. But then she got into a heavy thing with her boyfriend and we all split. Women can be such bitches. They might as well have been married. It was such a bad scene that when we left there we stayed on this beach for a couple of days and really got blown away. It was about the only time I can remember any of us having any kind of heavy discussion about women. None of the guys my age want to get hitched. It's like too much responsibility. I mean, you'd have to have a steady job and well . . . deal with your own old lady.

Anyhow, I decided anybody I thought would be hip enough to be my old lady would be too hip to *want* to be my old lady. I mean, that's one of the fatal attractions of this place. You can just ignore the women here until you want them for something. And lots of women come here. I mean, not just from this town. Like two girls will get in a car and drive for forty-five minutes to get here and then they'll wait on line and like after another forty-five minutes they'll get in and then they buy their own drinks and hang around. If you talk to them they are really flattered or something. If you feel like getting laid maybe you can pick one out and work an arrangement and then you do your thing and then maybe you never see her again and if you do it's like no big thing. You know, no responsibility for either side. No hassles either. In this whole social scene there is no require-ment to be a pair so you just do what suits you, or what suits your urges. I think the pill and this Women's Lib thing is just great for a guy like me. I mean, no obligations. They can take care of themselves.

I guess if I ever marry, which I probably won't, but if I ever did I wouldn't want her to work, though. I mean, she should take care of the kids and that stuff. Kids, now there's a really heavy trip. I mean, can you see this gooey little kid looking at you for everything he ever wanted. Heavy. I guess it's easier for a girl. I mean, my sister is married to a doctor and they live in Connecticut. She just repeats my mother's trip. More or less. I mean, my mother went to this really great college and plays a great golf game. Her family was really rich so she had a lot of advantages for a lady her age, you see. And now she plays golf and is a volunteer and reads and stuff. I guess the only thing that's hard on her is that she is the "family fender." She's right in there between my father and us kids or between us kids and us kids. I mean, she keeps it all down. Few hassles, little noise. I think she's too refined to like noise anyway.

We moved to this place when I was in the sixth grade from another town about ten minutes away from here. My dad isn't around much because his company is in Jersey and he drives a couple hundred miles a day round trip. They didn't want to live near his job because they don't like Jersey and this place had good schools and good clubs and my dad had played golf here for years so, like, he does his commute thing. Of course he does it in this big company-owned Cadillac which he likes. He gets a new one every year. It's like one of his toys or badges. I mean, I don't know which one. He really is a great golfer though. He has won a lot of club tournaments and things. I guess he's ambivalent about me 'cause he'll be pissed and not talk to me for days and days and then he turns around and gives me a five-hundred-dollar set of golf clubs. Golf's okay. When he wants to talk to me about something heavy or something evil I've done he'll say, "Hey son, let's do a couple of rounds. I've got a seven-thirty tee-off time." Then, between swings he'll lay a rap on me. I mean, I think I could beat him but it's hard to concentrate on your swing when you're waiting for the boom to fall.

Anyway, I went from Vermont to a school in Boston and then I flunked out. My old man decided four colleges were enough for any one person and he gave me this toy diploma and now he always calls me "the graduate."

I finally settled down a little. I mean, he got me a job through one of the men in his foursome and now I commute to the city and do this sorta management job at this little print place. I mean, I'm usually in here from eight to ten during the week. I mean, I gotta get up to catch this early train and all. But on the weekends I really swing. I mean, I'm in here till closing and since I'm a regular if I really get swacked out I can just crash here in one of the booths. They are nice to me here. I mean, I run a tab here and I pay it up when I get paid and it averages about forty dollars a week. Which leaves me about fifty dollars a week for trains and lunch and dope and stuff. I mean, I don't need more than that. Living at home is cheap and my mother gets on a kick about twice a year about how raggy I look and so she takes me shopping and lays out the bread for clothes and I guess it's an okay life. I mean, I'm gonna be twenty-three and there's no rush.

Paul's attitude toward women was "take it or leave it." He had told us, "If you ask a chick to go to bed and she turns you down, it's no big thing. I mean, there's no ego involvement because there's no responsibility. After all, a lay is a lay and some are better than others."

The only current issue that seemed to have made any impression at all on Paul was the Women's Liberation Movement. Obviously, he didn't understand what it was all about. But he certainly used it to justify satisfying his own urges.

"I mean, no obligations. They can take care of themselves."

Paul and many of his peers view the long-haired, blue-jeaned girls that surround them as pleasure toys. They've had toys since they were young. So it's natural that they would have toys when they were grown.

9 Beth and Larry

BETH: "I guess I really liked college. Otherwise I wouldn't have gone three different places."

LARRY: "I love comic books. Such an art. I'd really like to get into that. Maybe I will."

We arrived at the three-story hotel. It was the first place we had gone that resembled a Western hotel. The manager at the desk asked what we wanted. We told him that we were looking for two Americans named Beth and Larry. He led us through a door at the rear of the building and we found ourselves walking through a barren courtyard. We approached what appeared to be an abandoned two-story building at the back of the hotel. Our footsteps were heard because Larry came out of the doorway.

He was a twenty-one-year-old we had met the night before. He took us into a room that was approximately twenty by twenty. It had two walls of windows. None of the windows had screens. Two single beds had been pushed together into a corner. There was a card table, one chair, and a wardrobe. In spite of the minimal furniture, the room looked very cluttered. Clothes were all over the place. Leftover food and articles of clothing were intermingled on the card table along with dirty dishes. Comic books were falling out of the wardrobe. Flies were everywhere.

On the bed lay a frail blonde with her back to us. The first thing we noticed were long legs sticking out of a pair of very short, very old, cut-off blue jeans. Twenty-year-old Beth rolled over and faced us. She apologized for not getting up. She said she was very sick and had been running a high temperature. Larry reached over and picked up one of the dirty glasses. He poured Coca-Cola into it and handed it to Beth. He helped her slide up in bed and propped her up with several pillows.

BETH: My name is Beth. I am from West Virginia. My folks moved to Akron when I was in junior high school. My father is a college professor and my mother . . . well, she's a social-worker type; but she's always home. I had an older brother who is a draft-resister. Dodger? And me. And a younger brother and sister.

I got into drugs in high school. I was in an honor's program with kids all older than me. And I didn't hang around with the kids in school too much; they were all . . . you know, straight. But I belonged to this church group and it was really fantastic. They used to have these rallies on the weekends, and I loved to go to those rallies. . . . It was a good excuse to get out of the house. We would smoke marijuana and rap all weekend. It was a great place for girls and guys to do their thing together without parents hanging over you all the time.

And then school. I got good grades, but I never really liked it. They were all . . . you know—well, have you ever been to Akron? It's real . . . plastic suburbia. I mean it's not even like that, I guess. It's like a real factory town. The rubber kingdom of the world. There's a lot of blue-collar workers and it's a dirty old city. And tacky houses. Tacky track houses. And it's a tacky track town. It's . . . depressing. That's what it is: depressing.

My parents always thought I was strange. As though there was something wrong with me. They sent me, in my senior year, to a psychologist. It was my mother's idea, really. My father didn't believe in psychiatry. He was always saying things like, why am I throwing my money away? Give me the fifty dollars and I'll tell you all your troubles. And he never really understood that I couldn't tell him. He resented it, I guess, my going to a shrink. He was always trying to get me to tell him what I was telling the shrink. And he used to take me there and drive me home and it was like paranoia-time. He always said he wouldn't let me go alone or drive alone because it was a bad neighborhood; but he really loved to do it because it was a time when he had me a prisoner in his car and he could say to me whatever he wanted or ask me whatever he wanted. And I couldn't get out. And one time he was really pushing me and got me very upset and when I got to the shrink's I like freaked out. I was falling apart and I told him. I told him that my parents were good people, but I just couldn't understand them and they just couldn't understand me. He said the best thing for me to do was to hang low because I only had a couple more months and I was going to go off to college and that it would probably get better. It made me feel better to know maybe he was right.

One time, when I was a senior, I had some acid. It was my senior prom. I was going with a junior although he was the same age as me. And I just wasn't into proms and all. It wasn't my thing. And my parents, they were bummed out because they wanted me to go to the prom and they were going to be chaperones and they were really excited by the whole thing. You know, rah, rah, prom. And I had some acid because I thought wow, wow, a party, and after the party, it would be a really good time to drop. And I didn't realize that they were going to sit around and really chaperone.

I was sitting there waiting to drop the acid and I guess it was about nine-thirty when I finally did drop. And nothing happened. I was really bummed out. Then I figured well, okay, so what. And there was nothing else to do. And my parents were still there. So I decided I'd go home to bed and go to sleep. I fell asleep finally and then I woke up about midnight and it was like wow. I was lying on the floor and the room was strobing around me and I got up and went to the window and everything outside was strobing too. And like I just had to get out. I just knew that I had to go some place else. And I did the old pillow in the bed trick. You know, putting the pillows under the sheets and pretending they were me.

I snuck out of the house. And it was a real freak-out trip. Because I remember walking past a store, it was like an art gallery and it was the time when Andy Warhol was popular, you know, like Pop Art. And it was set up to look like a supermarket. And there was this plastic lady pushing a grocery cart and inside was a plastic baby and the cart was filled up with food and I was convinced that plastic people were ripping off the art gallery and I was sure they were seeing me and I was gonna be a witness to this crime and they were going to have to get me. So I started to run. And I ran past this bar. All the drunks of Akron were like hanging out in this park across from this bar and I passed them and they must have thought, look at this crazy girl running—let's chase her. Real scary. And I ran for blocks and blocks.

I had only one friend in Akron at this time. And I thought this was the best place to go while I was tripping. And I tried to get in his place, but no one came to the door. Then I was running up the fire escape. Banging on the windows. Let me in, let me in! He finally woke up and let me in and we talked and things were cool. And we talked a little more and then he left me alone. And I just sat there with a sketch pad and waited until the trip was over. And then it was like five-thirty or six o'clock the next morning, and I figured I better go home because I didn't want to get into a hassle with my parents. And I got home. And I thought . . . oh, God . . . I can't deal with this, I'm not down yet. I snuck back in the house . . . and sure enough, there in my bedroom the covers were thrown back and the pillows were still there and I figured well, now they know.

So I went down to the basement and talked to the dogs for a while. They were really comforting, you know, at a time like that. And I was hugging them and they were licking me and they were like saying, it's okay, all right, come on now. And then I finally felt better and I figured I'd better go upstairs and face the music. And wow, it was a real freak-out. My mother was convinced that I had been out balling my boyfriend all night. And I tried to convince them that I was having a nervous breakdown. I showed them my sketch pad and I guess the stuff that I had done was so freaked-out they really thought well, this kid finally blew. And they sort of eased off. And they were all upset.

After that, they kept me at home. Wow, what a trip. My father. He wasn't going to let me out of the house again. That was it. I couldn't even go to buy groceries or anything, until I went to college. I was just going to have to stay in the house. And my mother was all upset. She was ashamed and what will people think. My friend told his parents what had happened. His parents and my parents were pretty good friends. His parents were really cool. They called my parents and said, ''You know, things aren't so bad. Don't be so upset. The kids didn't mean anything bad. You know, they should go out tonight or come over here and, well, they will sit here and we will watch them every minute and you won't have to worry about anything.'' And my parents fell for it. My mother would never have done anything to interfere with her social thing.

So, I went over to his house that night and it was really fun being with them.

My parents wanted me to stay in Akron, to go to college. My father was on the staff at this college, in physics, and he demanded that I go there. But it was a real no-place school. And I was not interested at all. I was going to go to Boston University. I ended up being in three colleges. I guess I really liked college. Otherwise I wouldn't have gone three different places.

So I was going to go to Boston and I couldn't wait. You couldn't talk to my father. All he ever knew was discipline. Art and stuff didn't have any meaning. And my mother was always going around telling me, oh, don't do this, don't do that, oh, my God. You could never reason with her, either.

I remember when my brother, one summer, just couldn't take it anymore. He knew he was going to be drafted and he made up his mind that he was going to go to Europe with his girl. He made me promise not to tell my parents. He was afraid they would stop him before he left. And . . . he was gone. My mother was hysterical. And she kept saying to me, do you know where he is? And I kept saying, no. It was hard on me, because I promised my brother that I wouldn't tell. Then I found out that he got stuck in New York because his plane wasn't leaving. My mother heard something through the grapevine because a lot of our friends' parents were also her friends. So she said, "Come on, tell me. You do know, I know you do. Please, I'm so worried, tell me, tell me."

So I finally said, "Well, I'll tell you but you can't tell father because I promised my brother and you just can't, you just can't tell." And I told her and she felt better then. But she told my old man. Of course. I guess I knew she would. She was always doing that.

So I finally went to college. And it really fucked my head because like, you know, well, if you know what Cambridge is like, a whole new population every September because they have all those schools. And it's really strange because all the locals, the truck drivers and all those guys, they hang around and wait and every September it's time to check out all the new pieces [girls]. See what you can get. And I had been there only a week and I had had these really bummed-out experiences. One time a truck driver even chased me. And these guys were always asking me, hey, you, wanna smoke some dope? And I'd go up to their room and smoke some dope and it was always this really heavy scene and they were all after something else and I was always fighting them off.

One time I was walking to school and I went through this park and this guy was sitting there and he says, hey, wanna smoke some dope? And I said, hey, you pig. And it was Larry. But I did sit down and I did smoke some dope with him. And he moved in the next day. That was three years ago. And we've been together ever since.

When I told my parents that I wanted to come here to Afghanistan, it was like a freak-out. They said no. I was going to come anyway. I guess they felt better because they knew I was going to go with Larry. At least I wasn't going to be going alone. And so we came. Me and Larry. And I wasn't going to worry. I don't expect to go home for at least a couple of months yet. But I think we're gonna leave here because it's too hot. We will probably go to Pakistan. Or Nepal. Or some place.

It's been interesting here though. Being here. We would have left a little earlier, I guess, except that I got dysentery and like I've been to the doctor and I hope it's not anything more. I guess we will wait another day or so and see how I feel and then get going. See if we can do business someplace else. This hotel is kinda crummy; but it's cheap. It's about $2.50 a night. Our last hotel was 40 afs [80¢] a night. But they only had rope beds and our backs really got swayed from them.

We've been away from the States for seven weeks. We like being away from the States, because the scene Larry was into was really a drag. And we were looking for a way to get out of it. When a friend of Larry's said, "Do you want to go to Afghanistan?" I said, "Sure." And here I am. Before that, Larry was in the wholesale food distributing business. His father has a whole company. And he was passing through Philadelphia, you know, and he ended up working for him. He started off as a truck driver. Then he was promoted to an office boy, and then his old man made him a salesman. But it drove him crazy. After about nine months, he just couldn't take anymore. We had to get out. So we decided to split.

Larry had been wandering around the room while Beth spoke. He had been making a half-hearted attempt at straightening up the room. He was looking for his hashish. He was stoop-shouldered and clean-shaven. He had been listening attentively to what Beth had been saying and broke in.

LARRY: And my friend . . . he said, "Hey, I'll give you some money and you go to Afghanistan and buy shirts and all that stuff and bring it back and we will go into business." And so I said, "Sure, man, I'll go do that." I got my parents to agree because we told them we were going to do business. And my old man said, "Yeah. Okay. Great. Do a good job." The whole thing. "Hussle fast and make your million before you're thirty." So we're here . . . trying to make our million.

It was obvious to us that Beth and Larry had a good relationship. They enjoyed their quixotic sense of humor. So did we. Their style of delivery conveyed their humorous attitude toward life, no matter what they were describing.

BETH: The place we lived in Philly was real crazy. It was across from a track and it was really funny because it was like cheap and it had two bedrooms and was only one hundred dollars a month and had this big yard and lots of trees and flowers. We rented it from this lady who had lived there with her husband when they were first married. And it was the upstairs of a shabby two-family house.

Sort of casually she says, "Oh, by the way, there's this lady downstairs and she lives there with her retarded daughter. She makes strange noises at times and that's why the last people moved out." So I figured, well, okay, some seven-year-old girl who is retarded and maybe I can sit down and play with her. And read her stories and all kind of nice stuff like that. Well, the old lady is about eighty and her retarded daughter is about fifty. And she's . . . like a *biiiig* lady. Like six feet. It was a real freak show. And we would hear these noises. "Ah, ah, ahhh. She's gonna kill me. An, ah, ah. Put down that knife!" This lady would run up the stairs and bang on our door. "Please, please. I'll give you ten dollars." And we thought, oh, man. Forget it.

One time, we thought, okay, we'll call the cops. But the cops wouldn't come there anymore. Apparently they knew.

LARRY: When we first met, in Boston, I was getting really bad grades and I was really into dope. And I was messing around. And everybody seemed to be getting bummed out all the time. And everybody was saying to me, okay, you're smart, you can do better than this. I knew this guy, actually a businessman, who had this shack with carpet and phones and all. And he ran this dope-dealing thing. He was famous and everybody knew him. I dealt a little while. Never hard stuff. Always pot. Sometimes you could pick up a little hash.

Anyway, I wasn't doing too well and I was going to drop out. My parents were all uptight and my father was always saying, "We have a friend and he can help you get a job." And he wanted to know what I was interested in. And I was interested in comic books and movies. And he said, "I have a friend in Hollywood, and he owns some kind of studio, maybe he'll give you a job." My father was always trying to fix me up with these jobs.

So they bought me a ticket to L.A. and I got to L.A. and I was going to straighten out. I got off the plane and it was a real freak show. Especially in those days. I think the smog over L.A. was the smoke from the pot and the hash being smoked. I didn't have a lot of money and I wandered around and I didn't have a car, which is terrible out there. I couldn't take it.

So I decided to see what was happening in Boston. I needed bread and I thought I'd deal a little. I got some grass and I'd have twenty rolled joints and I'd sit there and every so often I'd see a new freshman come by and I'd say, "Hey, wanna smoke?" And the freshmen thought it was cool. And I knew they would ask me, "Hey, where can I get some good dope?" Because freshmen are new in the city and they don't know what is going on. So I figured I could say, "Yeah, I got some dope." And I'd sell it to them.

And one day I was sitting there and I see this girl coming along and I said, "Hey, you wanna smoke?" And she said, "Hey, you pig." And it was Beth. And we've been together ever since. Just like she said.

It had always been a real freak-out with my old man because

he had made it big and he worked hard and my grandfather was a housepainter and he was always ashamed because he had these calluses on his hands. And this was always a sure sign that he didn't have a profession. And the heat was always really on me to have a profession, you know. We had a lot of money. And we had this big house in Philadelphia. It's like a professional house—you got to get a professional to mow the lawn, a professional to decorate the house. And we had all these books on the shelves in the library, not because anybody read them. They were there because the bindings all matched and they looked good and went with the decor of the room. And my mother walks around with three sets of eyelashes on. And she has help in the house but she's always got to supervise everybody. Make sure that everything is super neat. She'd even sort my homework papers. I'm sure she thought I was kinda nuts sometimes. When I'd talk to her, I'd say, hey Mom, wasn't that a really great movie? And she'd be sitting there, with her clothes on, and her glasses on, and holding a magazine, with a cigarette in her hand. She was like Supermother, Superwife. Super-suburbanlady.

Beth seemed to have a great deal of affection for Larry's family. She never spoke about them with the bitterness she applied to her own family. Somehow they were more approachable to her.

BETH: Larry and I had this second-hand camper once and we painted it and fixed it. And like his mother flipped out. We were gonna throw some mattresses in the back to sleep on and I had some Indian material to hang on the windows. But she decided it had to be fixed up so we could be comfortable. She got yards of black and white houndstooth check material. And would you believe it? She decorated that bus. Like everything had to match. Black and white bedspreads, black and white curtains, black dishes, *white* carpeting. It was a camper! A *House Beautiful* camper! When we left we drove down the street and she was crying and saying she was so happy she had made us comfortable. And when we turned the corner, we tore all the stuff down. We wanted it to be home. But of course she never saw anything wrong with any of this.

At this point Larry was smoking his second chillum of hash. He lay down on the bed next to Beth and offered her some. They laughed warmly.

LARRY: I'll never forget—she'd go off the deep end every once in a while. And when I had my Bar Mitzvah, they picked this thing . . . everything was camel. My kid brother was like eight then and they wanted him in a suit just like mine. And they didn't make those suits for little kids, so they ordered one to be made. It was strange. This eight-year-old kid had this two-hundred-dollar-suit on. Six months later it didn't even fit him. But he had to look really good for the occasion. There were hundreds of people. It was sort of a goof. We had this huge reception. And all the parents got drunk. Really funny. Super, super production. For months and weeks they planned. My father rented the hotel for the out-of-town guests. This big number: Larry's Bar Mitzvah. It was really incredible when they left. Each guest was handed a special edition of the Sunday paper with this big headline across the front: LARRY IS HUGE SUCCESS AT HIS BAR MITZVAH! Can you believe that? And I got more than three hundred gifts and I had to write thank yous. I always hated to write. I can draw. I can talk. And I can read. In fact, I read everything I lay my hands on, but I really hate to write.

So you can imagine how it was. Here was this kid and he's got to write all these hundreds of things and my mother set goals. Every day I had to do so many. It was really a drag, and I kept getting more and more behind. And one day she did this big freak-out. She just flipped and got hysterical.

And by then I was smoking dope once in a while and I would smoke dope so that I wouldn't have to deal with this bullshit. And she thought there was something wrong with me. She was yelling and carrying on. And I decided the hell with this. I didn't need this garbage. And so I ran away from home. I was going to go to New York, to the World's Fair. Of course I didn't make it. I got into Jersey and I was near Atlantic City and that seemed a lot closer than New York and I had never been there. And I got there, late, and I slept under the boardwalk and woke up the next day and I met some other kids. They sorta helped me out. Finally I called my parents and they came and got me. And my mother was all kinds of upset. Crying, you know.

Of course, they sent me off to a shrink. And this shrink kept telling me that I was really smart. I did that for a while. And I wanted to go to college. All that. My father thought that was cool. My mother thought I should be a lawyer. I was such a good talker, you know. She had this real Jewish-mother imagery. She likes Beth and all. But whenever we stay in her house, she knows all about us, but Beth and I still can't sleep together. My father didn't care. He just leered a little and said, "Don't upset your mother."

My father is pretty cool, actually. He worked hard all his life and he made his bundle and he would still like to make more. He's had a lot of trouble with his heart. During the Navy, when he was younger, he got rheumatic fever, and he had to stay in this hospital for over a year. He's living on borrowed time, and he knows it. He's gotten philosophical, especially lately. We get along. But he really wants to make his million. He's always telling me, "Larry, start young." Money is like power for them. It's everything. That's why it was so easy to con him into letting me come here. Because it was this business thing.

What I'd really like to do would be to write comic books. Would be fantastic. I love comic books. Such an art. I'd really like to get into that. Maybe I will.

Beth and Larry were a straightforward, amusing young couple.

We believed Beth when she said that she had liked college. We also believed Larry when he said he was interested in comic books. His interest was sincere if only because he was willing to carry across the world two large suitcases filled with nothing but comic books.

Almost all of the young people with whom we spoke expressed interest in creative pursuits, like art, writing, or movie making. But we never did see anyone actually working at it. We met filmmakers without cameras, artists without paints, writers without pen or typewriter, craftsmen without tools. Their interest in creativity served to rationalize how they lived. But if they were so smart, why did they need to rationalize at all? Could part of the problem be that they had little understanding of the self-discipline required?

Where were either Beth or Larry to get the self-discipline to apply themselves to their studies? Where was Larry to get enough self-discipline to really do comic book art? The idea of apprenticeship—sustained effort over a long period of years—was foreign to many of these young people. Success should be instant . . . like instant coffee or the instant TV dinner. Somehow, after years of telling them how smart and how gifted they were, parents and teachers had blunted the drive needed to make something worthwhile. We felt that these youngsters had not been taught the hardest lessons of all: humility and endurance.

10 Meg

"So what's the point? I always like to just wait and see."

Meg was standing in front of The Wishing Well jukebox. She had a quarter in her hand but couldn't make up her mind. Her eyes skimmed over the numerous song titles.

"Hey, why don't you go ahead and put this quarter in the jukebox for me? This is the best-stocked jukebox around. They should keep the lousy bands out of here. I'd rather listen to the box anytime."

Meg's long, straight, sandy-brown hair hung to her waist. She looked like a typical American girl. When she turned around, you could see the front of her colorful, hand-embroidered shirt. Like all the other girls present, she wore jeans and clogs. The only attempt that any of them made at individuality was in their varied, expensive, handmade blouses. Meg had just turned twenty.

I come here a lot. About every weekend, I guess. They have

95

good bands here on the weekends. Well, my friends come here, too. I come here because here is where it's happening. Yeah. I didn't even have to wait in line. I'm a regular. I don't know what my parents think about my being here. I don't know if they know much about it. I don't have to tell them where I go, anyway, even though I live at home.

I finished with school. I went two years, and now I'm working so I can travel. It's cheaper sleeping and eating at home. I've been around the States. Me and my boyfriend traveled all last summer, so I guess I'd like to see Europe next. At first my parents didn't know I was going with a boy. I said I was going with some kids from school. I don't mind lying to my parents. It avoids so many hassles. But it got too intense, I don't know, it was too hard not to let them know Ted was going. And other kids' parents would have told them, maybe, so I finally told them. They were upset. At first they said I couldn't go. But I talked to them, and I explained how practical it would be to have him around; you know, the safety and everything. So they finally said okay. They still were not happy, they even offered to send me and my sister to Europe. I think it was the first time my father realized I'm not a little kid anymore.

I don't mind living with my parents now. I work during the day, and I go out at night, so they don't hassle me much. We don't do much together, I guess. I don't know, boating maybe . . . my father has a boat down at the club. He always wants me and my sister to go sailing them him, but we don't really like sailing. I'd rather go with some of my friends whose parents have a boat, you know, a cabin cruiser. And we can sit around and get wrecked and relax. With my father you can't do that! I don't know if they know we smoke . . . I guess they must suspect. But I wouldn't tell them. If they knew, they'd feel like they had to do something about it, you know, talk to us about how we're going on to heroin and we're going to have retarded babies. Anyway, I don't smoke that much. I have taken hallucinogens only twice . . . someone had some mesc, and I took some with them. I didn't like it that much. Like it lasted for nine hours, and I got sick. That stuff scares me some anyway. I mean I don't want to get my brain fucked up.

Meg asserted several times that she did not smoke very much marijuana. However, she got up and left the bar on a number of occasions. She would tell us not to go away, that she would be back in a minute. She told us later that she was out in the parking lot toking with one of her many friends. She must have done this five or six times in the course of an hour.

Oh, if my parents knew I took mescaline, they'd be really upset. I mean they're pretty straight. My father works for this company that makes portable chemical toilets. You know the Woodstock concert, Jimmi Hendrix, Sly? Well, his company supplied all the toilets for that. I couldn't believe it when I heard it. My sister and I got to go on the helicopter that was bringing those toilets. And when we landed we went behind the stage, and we got to listen to it all there. And we met some of the stars.

I don't know what my father does. Not exactly, I mean. He makes sure that the company runs smoothly, I guess. He works pretty hard. To relax he plays golf at the country club. He's good at golf; he likes it a lot. He plays just about every weekend in the summer. My mother plays too; she plays with the ladies' tee-off team. They go and golf all day and then they have dinner with friends at the club or something. I don't know that much about what they do, really; like I said, I'm out a lot.

If everyone is around, we have to eat at the same time though. My parents are really fussy about this. I guess they figure it's the only time we're together as a family. They're right, I guess. But I don't enjoy it that much. It gets harder and harder. We don't always see eye to eye and dinners get quieter as my sister and I get older. There just isn't that much we can all talk about that we all care about and don't get into arguments over. I guess my parents try, but it's hard. Sometimes my father asks our opinion of politics. My sister and me, we don't talk about politics that much. Politics doesn't really interest me. It doesn't really affect me. They're going to do whatever they're going to do, whether I care or not. I can't do anything about it. So why should I care? What concerns me are things that happen to me, in my own life. My parents voted for Nixon. I don't know how they feel about that now. No, I haven't been keeping up with everything on Watergate. I don't really follow it. I was for the kids who went to Washington. I didn't go though. But I signed a petition once at school. I don't know what happened to that petition.

I liked school okay. It was better than high school because you made up your own schedule and didn't have to be there all day. Classes were pretty boring sometimes, but there was one English class that we read some good poems in. No, I can't remember the names, but they were good. I hated writing papers, though. Or dissecting the fetal pig.

The boyfriend I went across the country with, his name is Ted, and we were pretty much going together. I saw him for almost three years, but now I'm seeing other people. Well, this girl, this Finnish girl who came here for the summer as a mother's helper, she started coming in here. And Ted started seeing her. Then he told me he wanted to "stop going out for a while." I knew it was this Finnish girl and I guess I was pretty uptight. I mean, I know Ted's no saint, I'm pretty sure he made it with other girls from time to time when we were going together but nothing big. But he wanted to see her instead of me, and I was kind of upset. But now I don't care if I never see him again. I mean, he can take his "for a while" and, you know . . . I don't care. Yeah, I've been seeing this guy named Jimmy. He's a good friend of Ted's, too. Yeah, I like Jimmy. I see him a lot. I see other people, too. I mean, it's no great big thing, but it's nice.

I'm twenty now. I don't know, I guess I'll get married sometime. I'd like to have kids. I really like babies a lot. Well, if my husband had a good-paying job, then I might not want to work. If I had kids I'd want to look after them. Working is a drag! I mean, I can think of better things to do than be some guy's secretary and type all day. Well, I'd see my friends during the day, I guess. We'd do things together . . . I don't know, have lunch. And at night, my husband would be home. And we would do things with our friends. There are some things I want to do first, like go to Europe.

I read some. I guess my favorite thing to read is short stories, because with big books I start to read, and then, you know, I go away and I never get back to the book. And I like movies.

My father? He makes I guess about forty, fifty thousand a year. He does all right, I guess. But it's not that much either; I mean, some people in this town make a couple of hundred thousand a year. Our house is nice; it has a swimming pool we put in and everything. It's nice because I can have my friends over and swim when my parents aren't there. No, they don't care. They never have said anything. Well, once some of my friends got pretty fucked up, there was a lot of wine and grass, and they threw some furniture, some chairs, in the pool. My parents were pretty upset, and they said I couldn't have any more parties. But then a week later I asked them, and said I would make sure nothing like that happened, and they said okay. So nothing happened, and it was all right. That was the only time they got upset.

I do think they would have liked it if I'd finished four years of school. They wanted me to stay and they would have paid and everything. But I didn't want to. I mean, what's the point? I can probably get just as good a job with two years of college as with four. And I wouldn't have known what to major in anyway.

I think my parents think I'll get married. I guess I will. Marriage is all right, but I wouldn't mind living with somebody first. That might be a good idea. But it would be hard for my parents to accept it. I think if you want kids you should be married, because it would be hard on the kid if people said, "Look at you, your parents aren't married."

I would want my kids to be happy. I would want to give them a nice home. And I would take them places and do things with them. And I'd want to talk to them and know how they're feeling. And I would try not to hassle them about things. But there would be certain things I would not let them do, either. I mean like steal, or wreck up somebody's house, or hurt somebody else.

Where I'd want to live? Oh, I don't know. Probably around here. I've lived here all my life, and I like it here all right. I like to travel and see other places, though. That's why I want to go to Europe. After that? I don't know. Maybe I'd go back to school, if I could decide on something to major in. But I don't like making plans in advance; they never seem to work out the way I plan them. Because they just don't, that's all. Things happen, things get in the way. So what's the point? I always like to just wait and see. Then I decide what I want to do. Then I can judge the situation.

We asked Meg what her plans were for the rest of the evening. She told us she had none. About an hour later we saw her by the jukebox again. A young man with a drink in his hand walked up to her.

"Hi, what's your name?"

"Meg."

"Want to get fucked?"

"Let's just wait a little and see."

11 Lloyd

". . . the family has failed to communicate any sense of community, any sense of importance, purpose, reason for being. The family has been caught up in what we call the 'Great American Rat Race'."

Lloyd and his wife, Sue, set up halfway houses in Mideast and Eastern countries. They run one themselves. The houses are for youngsters who are hooked on drugs and want to kick their habits, or ones who are sick and lonely.

Lloyd and Sue had become involved in this type of work partly because of their religious commitment to Christianity and partly because they felt that the most meaningful thing they could do for young people was to act as a kind of surrogate family for those who needed and wanted help. Thus they visited young people in prisons, nursed them through illnesses like dysentery, and helped them with their personal conflicts and emotional problems.

Lloyd is a minister. He had developed an interest in this type of work as a result of crisscrossing the United States over a period of two years, living with American families, and talking about drugs before high school and college audiences. What he saw appalled him. As he recounts in his interview, he saw a tremendous number of young people who were social casualties. Drugs were not only prevalent, they were practically universal. And youth experimentation with drugs had reached down in many instances even into the grammar school.

Lloyd felt that the answer to the drug problem was directly related to the disintegration of the middle-class family and the decline of Christian spiritual values. He believed that Americans needed to return to their basic human roots through sharing, affection, communication, giving. If anything then, Lloyd, while not optimistic about the possibility of a resurgence of the family in the United States, believed that without such a new commitment our social problems would deepen and most of our youth would be lost.

Lloyd related the Vietnam War, Woodstock, the Kent State murders, and the whole panoply of social events in the decade of the sixties to the plight of young people trying to define themselves, their identities, their lives in a violent society. He helped us to understand some of the basic factors that conspire to create the alienation, disavowal, and rejection that we saw amongst many of the young people.

We were going to go to India to open a house, open our home so to speak, to help young people. My wife and I were there in 1970; we were impressed with the needs of young people and wanted to identify with them and become involved in their needs. The only way we knew to do this was to stay in India and become students, so I enrolled in Benares, India University. I was going to study about six hours a week on a master's program and then we were just going to open our home and help kids in Benares.

I had prior experience working in Haight-Ashbury with kids who were strung out on drugs. I worked in a program called

Teen Challenge, and felt a real identification with the people that were strung out.

Generally, most kids abuse drugs because of some social-spiritual reason—search for identity, search for love, for security . . . There's also a desire to abuse drugs simply because of peer pressure. The third reason would be the existential experience—the thrill of getting stoned, the trip itself.

Most drug programs that are geared to treat kids who are desperate on hard drugs and want off, are physical programs. By that I mean they are hospital-oriented, bed-oriented types of programs; and so when you have a physical treatment you get physical results. But the real problem of the hard drug abuser is not physical. The big problem is mental addiction. So once you get a person off drugs physically, then you have to fill the emotional vacuum.

We believe that to get a kid off drugs permanently he needs a kind of surrogate family, a family who will help him find himself, provide security and discipline, and spiritual guidance. The hedonistic approach to living doesn't work, and it doesn't lift people out of despair.

You have to be quite honest with kids. We tell them that we feel that they're significant because they have, in philosophical terms, a personal beginning. If I'm talking to a junkie I'm going to use his language. God created him . . . he was made in the image of God and he's more than just a product of time less chance plus matter. Therefore his life really counts because God made him.

In my experience in working with junkies, I've discovered the family has been caught up in what we call the "Great American Rat Race." Buying things they don't need to keep up with people they don't like with money they don't have. So when Johnny wants attention, you give him . . . you give him a car, or you give him a motorcycle, or a bicycle or some clothes, or some money. Do anything but give him yourself and it doesn't take you very long to figure out when people give you things that it doesn't involve the giver. So the impersonalness of the family has really turned a lot of kids off.

Also, I would say a good majority of American kids who experiment with drugs are middle-class suburban young people. They watch mom and dad, you know, swigging their cocktails, popping their pills every morning and every night, and it's kind of ridiculous, as Margaret Mead says, for the father to stand with a cigarette in one hand and a cocktail in the other saying, "Now Junior, don't smoke marijuana. It's bad for you." Junior, I think, has smoked marijuana. He doesn't believe his family really cares.

I believe, from my exposure to upper middle-class American young people, their parents have been very tolerant. In fact I've had many of them cry on my shoulder and tell me, "I wish to heck that my parents would care what I do." I spoke in a private high school in Los Angeles—it was a year ago in March—and I had those kids falling all over me because my big line was responsibility, but on their terms. One very, very rich young lady lived on a yacht with her parents, did anything she wanted to do. She told me she had actually gone through everything. She was sixteen years old, experimented with everything there was. She wished that her parents would have been a lot less tolerant.

Parents ask their kid: "What are you going to do?" Father and mother think that occupation gives identity. I think that the reason they think that is they live in a totally different world than kids today. I personally think that there's a different kind of barrier between young people and their parents than there's ever existed before in history because of the turmoil . . . this shift in epistemology. Before people have always assumed that there's been meaning in life but my generation has no longer made that assumption. I believe that my generation is the first one to no longer ask the question, "What is the meaning to life?" They're now asking, "Is there meaning to life?" And that shift is actually tremendous.

Look at my generation, for example, in the last ten years, you talk to people twenty-five to thirty years old and what they've done. Many of them have burned themselves out. They've tried Eastern religion, they've gone through health foods, they may have been a Jesus person, they've done drugs, they've had marathon sex. You name it. They've gone through all these little trips. Most people pack that into a lifetime, but they've crammed it into ten years. They find a temporary reason for living in hedonism—just living for themselves, moment by moment.

It's my impression that American kids are doing drugs younger and in great quantity. My dad lives in a small town in Tennessee and in that small town there are now kids in grade school who are popping pills . . . and that's Tennessee. It's not New York. It's not Los Angeles.

You know, I agree with the kids . . . hang the paper . . . hang the wedding ceremonies, the ritual cocktail parties, the confirmations, the Bar Mitzvah's, the graduations! Forget that stuff . . . that's not important . . . but what's important is our commitment to one another as people. Be committed to each other . . . not only through the good, but learn to go through the bad. All of us go through changes and we grow and it's necessary for us to share each other, so that by all the great dynamic changes, we learn to love each other. I think that's exciting. The challenge of it is just beautiful.

That which is destroying America and her children is not a theology; it is not an ideology, it's not a particular brand of politics; it's personal selfishness. So I see the hope for us being both personal and historical *in God*. In that sense I'm an optimist.

12 Jenny and Mark

MARK: "The biggest decision that my contemporaries have to make is whether to run or to stay and fight."

JENNY: "That's what I had to decide when I met you."

We were looking for twenty-one-year-old Jenny and twenty-two-year-old Mark. We had met them the night before with a group of other Americans. The next morning we found Jenny and Mark having breakfast. They were drinking freshly squeezed orange juice and eating fresh eggs and bread. They were seated in two big comfortable chairs pulled up near a low wooden table. It was cool in the shade of a beautiful vine-covered arbor in a garden.

Jenny looked refreshing and unspoiled. Blue lights sparkled as the sun and the shadows fell across her long dark hair. Mark looked big, strong, and totally relaxed. Jenny handed us both a big glass of orange juice and invited us to join them.

MARK: There is not much of an affinity . . . I do not feel much of an affinity between myself and my family. They are different. They expect different things out of life than I do. I love them very much. But they still live in a different world than I do. Like my older brother, he's in med school and he's married. My older sister . . . she's a year older, he's two years older. She's married, she has a kid. And, yeah, everything's very set and well organized, and everyone is always into doing. They know where they are going. I don't particularly know exactly what I'm supposed to know. So it's different. It prevents us from being really friends, you know. We love each other very much; but we're not friends.

Parents so often have mistaken ideas or impressions about things. About certain philosophies of life. How can they— when it comes to one of their own offspring—how can they stand back and listen? They can't.

JENNY: I have a completely different relationship with my parents. When I was younger, I was close to my father. It was a companion-type thing. But then I had to see them more as people—and I came to Europe with my mother. Then I got really close to her; and I was never close to her before. After a while, I wasn't close to my father at all. He had a mistress, and she dominated his life, I thought. I always liked her; but I wouldn't accept her right away. Because of loyalty to my mother, I guess.

But now I can accept her. And I accept my father for his needs. And I see how much happier he is, and how she has brought him out. But I've also seen my mother develop by getting away from my father. By working in Europe and not letting the divorce destroy her. She developed herself rather than feeling sorry for herself. She did things she would have never done.

MARK: Parents are so dumb on so *many* subjects. They don't *really* know. Like they don't understand drugs at all. I was a junior at college and somehow my parents found out that I was smoking grass. A lot . . . not a lot, but regularly, you know. And this is how they reacted. My father took a plane out and I met him in Boston for the night. We had a talk about it and he went back the next day in time for work . . . don't miss work. And we left it that I was not going to smoke grass any more and that was the end of the discussion. Since that day nothing has ever, ever been said about it. But I didn't stop smoking grass. It's hard to say if my father really believed I would.

At that particular time in my life I went through a lot of other changes as well . . . in terms of my very strict upbringing. Things broke loose at a particular time. I think a lot of it was misconstrued by him. He thought it was the result of drugs, not other important things in my life. Drugs were just one of a number of things. Like acid was mostly a pleasurable thing. Nothing bad. I was with friends. I believe that if you do drugs, you'd better know what you are doing. And you *can* be responsible, you know. Like, for example, if you take acid. If you are in any way emotionally unbalanced, at the time, you would be a fool to drop acid. And I think you should be with good friends when you are tripping. Because it's really nice. And every time that I have done acid, I've done it with friends. I've been very happy. And it was a good thing to do. I gained insight about myself. I think cocaine is a very nice drug, but I also think it is a very dangerous drug . . . actually, it's the most dangerous drug that I've ever done because, you know, it really is addicting. Like I did cocaine for five or six days in a row once, and when I had no more, I could feel my body freak out . . . but it was nothing, you know. It does something to your body. But that's all I've done. I have friends who have done like fifty pills in three days. But I've never done anything like that.

JENNY: I mostly smoke grass and hash. I've done mescaline. I tried cocaine, but it was very unpleasant. Terrifying, actually. It almost made me want to quit drugs.

MARK: I have completely lost my religious background. I've discarded that. And I'm angry about it, because I feel it stagnated my growth. I think it is all very negative. It was the teachers and the church itself. It's a very negative approach to life. You know, I think the teachings of Christ are really beautiful; but the church does not teach what Christ taught. It's a very different thing.

JENNY: I rejected a lot of it. Sometimes I don't feel so good about it. But I think that I did get some things out of it. It made me think about certain standards, you know. I don't like to hurt other people.

MARK: I would not want any of my kids to experience what I have experienced. I really think that the way the teachings of Christianity are implemented are very negative. I think you are always told *not* to do things. You are taught to be ashamed of your body . . . the sexual things. That's why I feel anger. Because where I am at right now, I don't believe that you should be ashamed of your body.

I believe in the great power of the mind, that your mind is capable of doing incredible things. I think schools could be better. I really respect the university idea, because it's a real center for learning. But it's very difficult to do that within the framework that they sometimes force you to work in. You can't learn about Afghanistan by reading or studying anthropology books. There is such a gap between the Afghani and the experience. You can't expect teaching to do the impossible. But I think it would be good in an anthropology course to travel for a year in Afghanistan and get some credit. I think that's a step in the right direction.

JENNY: It's like a history course where you can't relate it. It's just facts and books. It's not real. America has so many good points, but so often you don't really see the importance of it. Like geometry . . . where can you apply it to life? It's just not taught that way. You're just a student and this is a course you take now. That's all. Children, when they are younger, are made to feel that they need to read these books . . . to get something out of them . . . rather than enjoying them or wanting to read them. Or questioning. Or wanting to read a lot more. It's why people get into a profession and not even know how they got there. Or how it applies to them. I feel the only way to enjoy school is to completely abandon the goal orientation. You know, when I was in school, the thing that really turned me off was that the whole thing was very claustrophobic. You were a student. You were going to college. You can't do anything else. Such a drag. It's not learning. I don't know what it is, but it's not learning. When you get out you have a better chance to learn, to feel.

MARK: I got bites all up and down my back and arms from bedbugs. But here it just doesn't bother me. It's a good thing, maybe, because I come from a very material environment. I find this life here very comfortable. At school I lived in a real place, you know. You just can't get into Afghani life living at a fancy hotel. But then I don't think you can get into Afghani life living here either. Or at any hotel. Because having anthropological sensibilities, I've really come to the conclusion in the last four weeks that this whole thing is such a joke, you know. You travel through a country. But you don't get to know that country. You get to know the people at the gas stations. You have the restaurants. Or the hotels that cater exclusively to Europeans. Occasionally you get to talk to some people. But to actually know what they are like and how they live—like in this country—you can't do it. The girl has a better chance because she has the possibility of going into the homes. It is just impossible for a man to do that here.

If you are traveling in the East and you are worried about the flies, and the dirt, then forget it. Don't come. You wake up in the morning and your face is covered with flies. You just can't let it bother you. So what if you do get bites on your arm—they go away. It's just not that important. Sometimes it's uncomfortable, but you just forget about it. In India things are going to be a lot worse. They'll be a lot dirtier . . . the food will have a lot more germs. I really begin to understand what an aseptic society is. I don't know when I had my last hot shower. I can't remember. There's no reason to take a shower every day. We take a shower every other day, every third day here. That's plenty. Always cold. I took two showers a day when I lived in the States.

As for sex, there are lots of opportunities in high school, you know, very natural . . . going with a girl for a while and just getting more and more involved. But not a big heavy rap. Nobody bothered me about it. I was a boy. But no one really wanted to know either. You know, even now, I wouldn't even bring it up! There's no use causing an earthquake when you don't have to.

JENNY: Well, my parents' reaction would be a lot different than yours. After I'd been living with somebody for a while or traveling with them my parents would assume I'm not going to change just for them. They'd give me a room, give us a room. It's not like your kid goes out one night and brings home someone and has lots of different sexual experiences all the time. You know what I mean? You'd kind of question the depth of their relationship. I think when I was younger, they wouldn't have liked it very much, but as I get older I think my parents would see that we're old enough to make up our own minds. If you expect your parents to be friends, you have to help, too. I never would have made friends with my parents if I hadn't made the effort or been open and loved them. I wanted to travel with Mark and told them about it. The initial reaction of my mother wasn't very good, but she accepts it now.

When my parents contemplated divorcing, they explained it to us. Our parents wanted to hear what we had to say. They didn't want us to be screwed up by keeping a lot of feelings inside. They said to tell them even if it was negative. I tried. It was hard so I wrote a very long letter to my father telling him to consider a lot of things. It was sort of a surprise to me. But I felt so strongly. I also realized that, no matter what I said, I wouldn't influence him, 'cause he had made his decision.

My parents were married twenty years and then my mother

came to me and told me about it. She had heard that my father was interested in another woman and my mother found out and discussed it with my father and that was when the divorce thing was considered. My father lived with this woman for four years before he married her. For a period of time before that my father's mother and my mother and everybody was condemning it and making me feel uncomfortable. And that was another reason why I wanted to stay in Europe, because they were all living in the same community so it was hard.

I never thought that he would get married again, you know. And in a way it makes me question whether I would really ever want to get married. Whether I see the purpose of a license and all the hassles that are involved.

I think kids feel less guilty now because they're experimenting around more than their parents; the parents were trying to stay within the social framework and be accepted.

I wonder if affluence helps the quality of life. The tendency is when a youth comes from an affluent family, there's more chance that he can get a supply of drugs of any sort, or pick up any deal, or whatever. I also think that a lot of young people see that the American Dream is not anything worth getting excited about. Who really wants to live in a suburb like the Joneses and the Smiths . . . having to crawl in bed every night, needing a car for him to go down to the sterile office and, you know, she turns into a mommy for eight hours. And he comes home to a bitchy wife and kids. For a kid it's pretty good most parents think. When you're going through grammar school it's very comfortable. You have a lot of friends. If you live in the suburbs, presumably your family has enough money so they can provide you with material things. When you're a kid, I guess material things, they're important to you . . . to have a nice bike, or whatever.

MARK: I would never raise a kid in the suburbs because I couldn't stand it. I don't think it's good. But as a kid I didn't think about those things. As a kid you just go riding your bike on the block, getting an ice-cream cone. It wasn't just the suburbs.

It was the whole thing, you know. You're upper middle class. If you're an upper middle-class family you live in the suburbs. Your father works in the city. Your mother is a housewife. You go to a private school. Of course that shapes you. The way it affected me negatively was that when I got out of college, I didn't know what the hell to do. I knew I had to do something because now school was over, and now it was time to do something. I was ready for something, and I didn't know what it was. Which is absurd, you know. All the frustration I put myself through because of these hang-ups, these prejudices that I acquired from my upbringing. It really strangled me a lot.

JENNY: I wasn't in that predicament. As far as the marriage thing, I was never pushed into it. Even when I grew up my parents never made me believe that I had to be a housewife. I think it was more of a "do something with yourself" kind of thing. And if you do that the other will come later on.

MARK: We also look at things in terms of, "Is this worthwhile?" You have to if you're going to put some order in your life. What is good about living in the suburbs? About having a job? Making a lot of money? Is there anything good about it? My parents are very devout, you know, so they get their fulfillment in life through their religion. They use it as a crutch, and they're very, very happy. It works for them, not necessarily for me.

JENNY: I think suburbia offers more security to a lot of people. People our age, even if they deny it now, when the time comes, their friends will be living in certain areas, and the question will come up, "Why shouldn't we live in that area, too, and be with our friends and send our children to school with our friends' children?"

MARK: The biggest decision that my contemporaries have to make is whether to run or to stay and fight.

JENNY: That's what I had to decide when I met you!
[Laughter]

MARK: That's what I say. That's why I feel it would be a
whole lot nicer and easier to live up in northern Wisconsin
somewhere. Just living a very simple life and just being happy.
But people are limited by certain things that you can do in terms
of an educational background. And where you are able to do
something you can do. And is it worth doing? It's hard for me to
know the answer to that.

JENNY: So often I see marriage or relationships or family
things as a habit. And people get hooked. They say to themselves at different times of their life, "Well, why should I leave
this nice environment? I'm fairly happy in this environment."
You get accustomed to the ease of just sending your child down
the street to the public school. Supermarket's right down the
street. Maybe it should be like traveling. When you're moving
around and forced into a situation, you have to adapt . . . be
much more extroverted, make new friends, move into new
things. You've got to be more flexible. I think it's better for kids
to experience different things. I think it's better for parents, too,
to move around. Why should they be stuck . . .

MARK: Hedonism is a strong word. And it's used about
our generation, but I don't think it's applicable. I very much
believe in individual freedom and, as far as social obligations, I
don't believe that I have an obligation to anyone. But I do
recognize the suffering and that I have been provided with
certain advantages, extraordinary advantages in terms of greater choice, and I can see that now where I couldn't see that before
I came here. I don't know how to incorporate this type of
philosophy with my life. I think that the most important thing is
not a pleasurable life, but a good life. Hedonism is always
seeking pleasures and things. I don't mean that. I mean a good
life; being a good person. That's how I think you can alleviate

human suffering. You can be a compassionate human being. I think sharing . . . showing sympathy toward others.

JENNY: I agree with what he said. You don't have to do the big world number. Just give of yourself. You can give a lot of money—a lot of parents do that, or a lot of organizations do that for social causes, but they give very little of themselves. I think if you can share more of yourself and what you have in a daily sense, that's socialism in a way.

MARK: I saw a very interesting thing yesterday, down in the old bazaar. There was a very old man walking down the street. He was a beggar. And one of the guys I was with gave him five Afghanis, which is a lot to give him. You know, the most you usually give is one Afghani or half an Afghani. Anyway, what the guy did—he was just stooping over, walking along—when he saw the money, he stroked his beard three times, thanking God, praising Allah. And he just kept on walking, didn't even look at the person who had given him the money. And that type of thing is a real gift. He really appreciated it and it was a very meaningful thing.

Just ten minutes ago we were walking on the sidewalk, and these two kids, this one girl and this guy, Americans, came up to us and gave us this really long rap about how they were stuck in Afghanistan; how they needed money, you know, and wanted us to give them 100 Afghanis, you know. For some reason I just felt no compassion toward them like I did toward the old Afghani because they were just really misusing their intelligence. They were very stupid people. They had gotten themselves into this situation. I think they were lying, but if it were true they were just handling it in a very stupid way and I didn't feel at all like giving them a cent . . . and I didn't. But the old man really appreciated this gift that was given to him.

JENNY: It happens so often that you want to give it to all of them. But then I heard in India that there's so many of them, that you'll end up being on line with the beggars if you're not careful. So there is a limit.

Of all the young people we interviewed, Jenny and Mark were certainly the least involved with drugs. They are the kind of people most parents would feel comfortable around—until you listen to them talk. We discovered that they had contradictory feelings about many issues.

For example, even though Mark enjoyed his childhood in suburbia, today if he had children, he would not want to raise them there. Or again, sometimes Mark seems to assert his faith in schooling and yet at other times he disavows the framework of the school itself. Surely they were ambivalent about so many things and profoundly uncertain as to how they would generate answers in their own lives. But at least they were constantly questioning.

13 Barry

"I don't have to look for meaning in life. I don't think there is meaning in life. I think, you know, there are x/y chromosomes."

Barry was a college graduate from New York. He was the smart, aggressive son of a successful father. A politically aware twenty-two-year-old, he was experienced in sex, drugs and business. We sat in the garden. The unending rock music blared out at us. Barry wore plaid Bermuda shorts and a button-down Oxford shirt. Stoned out of his mind, he talked about his first million and how he would make it, how Afghanistan was a stopover for him, how he was taking time to formulate his plan to make a killing.

You form your idea of what you gotta do, based on your former experiences. For example, my experience with women . . . I always went out with older women. When I went to college I went out with maybe two college girls the whole time. I went out with forty-year-old women and women in their thirties. And I enjoyed it. There was this woman I was seeing. She had a son named Barry. He was sixteen. I was only eighteen myself.

She just dug me. One day she says, "You know, I wish you'd fall in love with me." Or something like that. Then you are sitting there and you say to yourself: "What am I doing here?" And you gotta run.

In college, I learned women. And I learned how to organize a little bit, but I must say that I learned much more in high school. They threw much more at you. More courses. Man, there were terms at college I might have had five courses, then I would drop one. And I wouldn't go to maybe three courses for three months . . . ever. And then sometimes I wouldn't even take the midterms. I would just show up for the final.

At the time, I was living at a fraternity. I was always moving around when I was young. My family did the whole route from being born in Manhattan to going to Queens and then going to Levittown . . . constantly getting better and coming back to the city and then having a house in the country. We lived in eight houses and maybe seven apartments in twenty years. In different towns. And that, I think, is no good. You have to have some sort of foundation. So, I always had no friends.

I decided that I needed something when I got to college. I decided that I wanted a fraternity; I just had to decide which one. I wanted a fraternity because I wanted to make some lasting friendships. And I didn't think that a dormitory was the place to do it. I wanted just a couple of good friends. And to that end I achieved my aim in the frat house and I also had a lot of good times.

But I must say that I went to college too early. I had a very high I.Q. when I was really young. We all do in my family—my brother, too. And my parents wanted me to go to college early. I went into parochial school when I was four. Then they wanted to skip me in the third grade but I was so young that it was just no good. It's no good to go to college when you are too young.

There was no question that I would go to college. It was not a matter of my motivation. In the end, it was a matter of my parents and there was a matter of completing something that I had started. That was all the motivation that was there. For me there was never a question of me getting a job. I was never gonna get a job. I am being groomed for better things than that.

I said to myself: I can't get a job and I can't hold a job and I refuse. Instead I went in another direction. The direction of going into my own thing, investing or gambling. You know, I made a great deal of money in playing the horses and then lost it all. I learned a lot from that, too. I learned that I can't go near the track. I was into harness racing. I just went from betting three hundred dollars to four hundred to six hundred dollars a race. I went back and bet ten, five, two dollars. And, you know, I got enjoyment out of both. I have this dream to have the largest stable in Yonkers Raceway. I love horses. It's just like when I go to Las Vegas, man. I went to Las Vegas with my last thousand dollars. Hit it on the red, because I like red grass.

And I won and then I lost. It was my fault. My friend was visiting me and he kept making me bet more. And I should have known. I should have walked out but I felt too exuberant and so I said okay, fuck it! And there it went.

Besides the women and gambling, drugs was the other major thing in college. Yes, everybody gets into drugs in college. Drugs are just a natural. People have money. And dealing is natural.

I was reared on Panama Red—the finest grass in the world. There was a constant supply. We would cop from Puerto Ricans downtown. They would be supplied by the policemen, you know. It was unreal.

At first, I didn't want to get into anything else. But things come up. And sometimes your head happens to be in the right place. Like we have a country house upstate, about fifteen acres, mostly forest. A friend comes up and gives me this tab of mescaline or acid and it's the right time, you know . . . you do it. It's pleasant. Sometimes it's unpleasant.

The first couple of times I was really scared of acid. Acid is really heavy. Mescaline . . . you take a couple dozen trips of mescaline and it's nothing. It's really nothing; very mellow. It's just feeling great. You want to make love to the world. But LSD . . . you are a little bit frightened. I had one bad experience up in the country where I just took one and I didn't get off too well. So I took another one a half an hour later. Another one, another one. I took maybe four. And this guy I was with was really into downs and acid. So we took a couple of Libriums. And some Valium and some Seconals. I sort of . . . well, it wasn't me anymore. There was no ego. And I didn't know which was me and which was something else. It made me jittery. I was always not sure if I was all there. You are just not sure. I slept for forty hours . . . and after that, I woke up and I felt just great, you know. Wow! I'm all there! So after that I just had no fear. At all. Like I've had mild times on LSD. In Kabul I had . . . like, man, I can't say revelation. Revelation is the wrong word, man. I could say total euphoria. I could say total contentment in an artificial way. An evening when everything is funny, to the point where you hurt the next day because you're laughing for ten hours. Constantly laughing. It's fantastic. And like acid is great for sex, too.

And then there's psylocibin, which I think is better than LSD. It's just an incredible sensory drug. You have an awareness about you. You can tell when people are coming in from another room. You have a tentacle out. You play music and you see notes in the most incredible colors. And sex . . . well, sex with psylocibin is just for me, well, it's spiritual. It's a physical spiritual. Ecstasy. A long time.

I smoked in college, too. I never got into ups and downs. I *hate* ups . . . because I had to take diet pills when I was younger. I don't like downs either; they just make me dizzy. So I stayed away from that.

And then came the real dope. At college. Smack, with all my friends in New York, that's all dope is. When you say dope you are talking about heroin. I was scared stiff the first time I snorted it. I just threw up and it was nice. And I was scared, no doubt. And then you get into the whole psychological thing that you have to throw up because it's evil. I mean it's just too much. But I just watched half of my friends disintegrate.

But I never fixed. Leave that to my brother. He'd fix people up. It didn't bother him at all. It bothers a lot of people, you know. What bothers you is that you have a friend that you've known for three or four years—gone through college with him—and he's sitting there like this . . . putting twenty holes in his vein. It's really bad, you know.

I never shot up. But, man, cocaine is fabulous. Just beautiful. I don't do that to excess either. You can't OD on coke. But I'm careful, man, with all opiates. Like nobody in the States knows about opium . . . I had a couple of bouts here. They have no idea about it. But you come here and wow! A piece of opium and you eat it, and wow, you die. Right. Someone I knew had an opium party and would hand out a piece and you would eat a piece with everybody who came; by the end of the evening, everybody was out dead, you know what I mean. But like this cat was out dead dead. He ate like ten grams. And you are supposed to eat maybe half a gram. I eat a gram, maybe three-quarters of a gram.

Opium is like heroin. Some people like it better because it's lighter. Opium first of all makes you a little nauseous and dizzy and you shouldn't be going too many places. Just lie down. Like it's total contentment. It's a dream drug. Just going off on beautiful dreams. And the whole thing is just beautiful. But it's a drug that you got to respect, you know. I haven't always respected it. I got very sick. I just felt like I wanted to die, you know. But I'm the kind of guy that does it when it's around. I am also on a diet thing . . . like I've been on every diet known to mankind. But I'm not a junkie or anything like it. I'm just setting it down for the record, you know.

Just before I came to Kabul I was wholesaling and jobbing Turkish coats and Afghani coats and all sorts of clothing. I was a traveling salesman. But I had my own business again. I couldn't just be a commission salesman. I had to go out and find a partner and put it together and go and get the stuff and sell it myself. And if I make it, it's mine; and if I lose it, it's mine. And, you know, I'm not making money for some prick who is sitting behind a desk. I make it for me. I can't stand to make it for somebody else.

When I am doing something really important, no weed, no drugs. Nothing. Because the only way I am going to get ahead, especially in my field, is to put my brain against the best, you know. And you can't do that when you are stoned out. Not on Colombian. No way.

There are two things that are really important to me right now. And in terms of a long-term thing they are equal. One is friendship. And I mean loyal friendship. And the other thing is my drive for success.

I have a tremendous desire for a great deal of money. The money will get me a lot of things, you know. For everything that I've wanted, I figured it would cost around ten million dollars and a million dollars a year, plus . . . yeah, about that. That would be houses all over the world. Don't you understand, man, some people are into the Monopoly Game. I know that I am good at it. I know that I could be great. But you can't say you are great and still be in Afghanistan. It's deluding yourself.

I want to make films. Produce, man. Executive produce. Fitting the pieces together. Man, I love it. I crave it. The deal. The deal. Pitting my brains against the union. Just sitting there . . . I love to sit there and manipulate people. I love it. I dig it. I always love jigsaw puzzles. I could sit down for two days until I finish a jigsaw puzzle—not take my eyes off it—'cause I love how it fits together.

I was always told that I was brought to a one-room flat in Washington Heights and the bathroom was shared with a Puerto Rican family in the hall. Right. That memory—it's not a memory—that picture was enough to start me. My father was a spiritual leader in the community. Like he marries people now because they are in trouble, or because they are a Catholic and a Jew and there is nobody else they can go to. People are always coming to him for advice. Intelligence and wisdom was, you know, thrown into me. (And like I don't know if astrology has anything to do with it, but I'm a Taurus.) My father always instilled in me that it was never important to have a million dollars. He tried to, right. He never thought that he would make it. Or he had these doubts because he started so late. He had this religious thing the first half of his life which screwed him over. And he cut me down when I told him about my drive, you know . . . when I told him that I was going to have a million dollars by the time I was twenty-five. Well, he told me that I would not have a million. It made a knot in me. I'm gonna make it. I know it.

School is a waste of time. It is, man, for me. I'm a businessman. I've read more in the five months that I've been away than in my last year at school.

I learned how to work hard in New York. I spent ten years all over the South Shore of Long Island. And then I escaped soon enough for my sanity. I went back to Manhattan. My parents pulled me in there, 'cause I was in too many Jewish ghettos. They said, "That's not how you are gonna go through life. There's more to life than Jews, you know. And you can't stay in the South Shore all your life. You go back to the city and . . ." It was a fabulous experience. I don't know if I want to live in New York. But I am sure glad I came from there and grew up there.

The people on Long Island. The people are empty. Just total . . . total people of the buck. Like I'm a proud Jew. There's been such disintegration of values where I lived. And friendships were very hard to come by there because the people were always buying. Parents and children alike. It was really an incredible scene. When I was around eight or nine years old, they had birthday parties and the parents promoted matches for future marriages. And my parents had a little bit more money than the rest, so I was . . . prime. It was buying and the parents were in on it. And the chicks . . . they are completely destroyed . . . their heads are just nowhere. It was just a very bad environment in which to grow up. And that's why all the kids became junkies. Really. In New York you have no choice but to live on Long Island. Until you are sixteen you can't even drive a car. You can't go anywhere. You have to have your parents drive you. You live in a little community. And those communities are really bad. The parents . . . the parents are so frustrated that they turn to total materialism with the marble fronts and which one is better than the next. I always remember it because everybody around us always had marble and we never had any.

My father was a rabbi. He was brought up in Russia in his early years to be a rabbi. A very brilliant man. Orthodox. And his father was one and it was a whole thing before him. Then he came here and . . . like he was ordained the highest ordination that there is. He became a rabbi when he was like nineteen. But the hypocrisy became too great and he became a very successful businessman.

When I moved back to the city, I was the only kid I knew whose parents were living together. People tell me about suburbia, about the incredibly bad relationships they have with their parents. But my family is as tight as anything.

My mother is a great lady. She's into politics now. She got me into politics when I was really young. Like two years old. She was for Stevenson. She was standing on street corners and I was handing out buttons. And that was my entrance into politics. And I was always very fat, which increased my interest because I had no other interest. I would always have to hit the ball twice as far as anybody else to get to first base. I worked for Stevenson in 1960, trying to draft him, you know. For Kennedy, for Humphrey . . . and Lindsay the first time. I was even into giving speeches with loudspeakers and stuff. It was a tremendous trip. And it gave me a tremendous interest in the structure of government. I wanted to go into politics, especially since my family is so well connected in New York. But there is so much disgusting bullshit. Well, you know, things are happening which you think could only happen in Czarist Russia. Just incredible governmental persecutions. Bribery. Anything you can think of goes on in New York State. I could have told you the names of the judges to be nominated even before the constitutional convention was opened, because it costs at least $100,000 a judgeship. And it was all bought and paid for. It's that type of trip. It's people who have to buy and sell votes, man.

I had to make a decision if I wanted politics or not. Politics or money. And I wanted money more than politics. I have tremendous ambition. I am an empire builder. I want to build a financial empire. I've thought about it a great deal. Well, I started in business when I was eight or nine. I was into business. Like I could never hold a job for anybody. I did a whole thing with newspapers. And then I was in dozens, literally dozens of businesses. All through my teens, you know. I would manufacture little plastic molds. I went through the entire *Business Opportunity* magazine. I learned a lot of hard things about life. I went out and I was a traveling salesman. I was a door-to-door salesman. Selling light bulbs. All sorts of things. I learned the things you learn when you get out of college and go and get a job. I had all that when I was twelve and thirteen years old. I was always reading the stock market and stock market analysis. And business books. My brother, who is twenty months younger, was always into science fiction. I was fascinated by the stock market. I want to have a seat on the stock market. When I was sixteen I had my own mutual fund. I got my friends to give me money to invest for them. I did all this research and set up a company with all the rules and regulations. I really did a trip on it. And everything I did . . . I always registered a name. I always got business cards. You can walk in anywhere if you have a suit on and a card. I financed everything myself. Well, the first time I invested in the market, my father gave me enough bread to let me hang myself. Then he would come in at the end. Those ten-dollar gifts over the years would add up, you know. From different holidays. We invested in some private corporations. We would spend money . . . we'd spend $1,500 . . . we'd just go out and blow it. Then I blew the rest just on horses. Which was another period. But for me to make a business takes me about a minute when an idea strikes.

In two months, to get into my career, I am going to sit down with my father and we're together going to decide what's best for me. I'm not looking to do anything small, man. Some people don't want to do anything with their father. I consider my father an *incredible* man, just *incredible*. Absolutely. He's a religious guider. A scholar. And he knows a tremendous amount about business. A natural. And, in fact, another reason that I am so cocksure is because I have had so much tutoring from him all through the years. We would sit down anytime and we would analyze things . . . why this restaurant was doing well or why it wasn't. This type of thing, man. My mind is really attuned to this, you know. I was brought up with it. I'm not going to go into anything that I am not going to engineer. Dig? I've got a lot of opportunity that most people don't have.

I figure that my father started with nothing and he ends up wherever he ends up, man. I have to end up a lot further. I have a tremendous thing about that, you know. I was the first born and I have tremendous competition with my father, even though he doesn't want that. I want to prove to him that I'm as good as him and I want to do it before he dies. He's fifty-five. But there's been a lot of strain and one heart attack.

Man, this isn't a desire—it's a need. To make it.

When you want competition and you love someone intensely, there is some hate there, too. I believe in using what you got, whether it's your mouth, your contacts, whatever it is. Again and again, it's my old man. Let your mother lick the stamps, he says, you go in the backroom. So I'd make plans with the District Leader and get on certain committees. Important committees, not just ones that were interesting. Public relations committees. That's where politics is at. In New York anyway.

I'm going back to the States very soon. Take some time and play some tennis and some pool. And think. And discuss. It will take me a little while. I can't make decisions in August. So September will come. And then I will get into it.

I know what I want to do. I know that I want to make films. But I'm not gonna make films for somebody else.

My father is in films. And, well, I got distribution sewed up if I make the films. But I want to make a documentary first. I was really thinking about a documentary in Afghanistan. A real hard-hitting one, you know. I think they would really buy it. You can do it for about $75,000. Low budget. Move your

money up fast. You don't have to wait. No shit. I've already
made one short. I have my own production company in L.A.
My company did a fantasy film. We shot it in the National
Forest in California. It was well shot. My father made a movie
and I was working on the movie. And the assistant director and I
got together and we formed our own company. It was fantastic.
I also worked on a TV show . . . documentary and a couple of
other things. Fantastic, a fantastic business. So volatile. And
so, so exciting—especially if you can do it at the upper level.
Making films and smoking—that's where it's at.

We smoke around the house all the time. One of my father's
key movie stars would come up to the country and we would sit
around discussing his part in the next film—very, very serious
discussions, you know, you have a million dollars on the
line—and the joint would be passed around. And my brother
would take a toke, and then me, and the star would be rolling as
fast as me, and this cat would take a toke and pass it to my
father, and my father would pass it to my brother. Right on with
this rap. Incredible. Just very very cool.

My mother has smoked. We turned her on. My father
smokes. He smoked in the thirties. He said it was nothing;
you'd go in a bar and somebody would hand you a joint. But
he's a Corvoisier, man, I'm sure. A different trip altogether.
And my mother . . . I think she'll get into smoking when it's
legalized. She has this paranoia trip. But she's really fantastic
with gin. She bubbles.

My father has his own thing. He reconciles Spinoza and his
life style and—I'll tell you, man, he's one of the few people I
ever met, which is why I respect him so highly, who made it
honestly. He made it because he created an industry for himself,
with the giants. He just carved it out for himself. It doesn't
happen very often. And there have been times when I've told
him, man, there have been times when he could have eased his
life, where it would have been easy, where he wouldn't have
had a heart attack. And it meant $25,000 cash. And I pleaded
with him: pay the bastard off. Governmental. These bastards.

He wanted to fight them in court. Fuck 'em. Beat 'em in every court in the state. That's the type of guy he is. You can reconcile being a businessman and doing that, man. Very easily.

There is this tremendous love-hate in my father, man. My brother and I have tremendous differences and yet my brother is my best friend—which gives you even more insight into our family. It's just so tight. But it's not a "Godfather" type thing. Tight, but totally independent. In fact, my father pays me for coming over here to Afghanistan because that's what I want to do.

Like if I would have been my brother's age, I would not have graduated. But I was the last straight guy, which was lucky for me in that I graduated. So I was older and looking down at my brother's class, which was completely stoned out. And they looked like derelicts.

My brother is convinced that he wants to go back to school. He wants to go into physics. He's settling down. But I don't know if I ever will.

Man is a polygamist in one respect: he will go after other women if he has one. But, man, I need one woman. I just love and cherish a woman. And she just cherishes me. I really don't need anybody else. But in terms of marriage, I can't conceive of marriage before thirty. Or kids. I might find the right woman tomorrow and live with her for the rest of my life, but I wouldn't marry her until I was thirty or thirty-five. For one thing, it's material, but it's also being tied down. That contract is so forever.

In this life you can do whatever the hell you want. Which is another reason why I want money . . . to do whatever the hell I want.

I *know* that I am going to be rich. Very rich. I am destined to be rich. I am destined to run an empire. Mini-empire, maxi-empire . . . I don't know what it is. But it's going to happen, you know. And if you have that kind of confidence that you can afford to go out and take risks, you know, the old American trip—I would really dig it. I would know that I got the backing. My trip is different because, like you say, I'm tied into my father and I would consider it a tragedy if he died because he's worth more to me alive than dead. I want to learn from him.

My image is to have a tremendously successful empire. I'm on a benevolence trip, too, a generosity trip with my money. Well, I have a very radical point of view on economics. I think there should be a ten or fifteen percent shift in the economy toward the workers. And in stock ownership. That kind of thing. Somebody works for me, I believe in paying him what he's worth.

Loyalty means a lot to me. I must say that. I've been nice, awfully nice, to a lot of people and too many of them have crossed me. Crossing me is taking advantage. For a friend to disgrace you in front of your peers is absolute disloyalty. It's treason, man. It's like cutting off a junkie. There's no sewing it up. It's stealing money out of your own pocket. Disloyalty.

The love-hate relationship in my family came because my mother and father were two incredibly strong and forceful people. Both of them coming down on you. Right. So when that happens you pull one way . . . you pull another way . . . you don't know which way to pull.

When I'm a parent, I'm going to let my kids be more independent than I was. But also I want to have just enough of authority so that they don't stray. So that I'm there if they need me.

My parents made a lot of bad mistakes, too. They fed me too much, they gave me too much, they made me a little bit too spoiled; but I'm basically a good human being, you know.

I'm not even very independent now. No. There's no way I could self-delude myself into thinking that I was independent. I am totally dependent financially but I can virtually make my own decisions. Sometimes I think I ought to make some money on my own. I should.

You can only feel yourself inside. You think. You rationalize. You put down. In your mind. And you say to yourself: this is what I want. This is what I want! If you think it's what you want, and not what your father wants, then you don't give a shit what anybody says, man. Some people have come to

me and said you are not yourself, man. Friends who are not
material. Friends who are preoccupied, shall we say, with
looking for meaning in life. I don't have to look for meaning in
life. I don't think there is meaning in life. I think, you know,
there are x/y chromosomes. You can live, you can work, you
can play. It's a different trip, man. That's all it is.

I have to live on my own terms. My father has tried to
influence my life, of course. And of course he's done a good
job. I know I want to be rich, man. I don't have to be, you know.
I know it. That's something that my father wants for me. And I
want it because he wants it. He doesn't really want to be rich,
man. I'm called the millionaire in my family, man. He's not.
I'm the one who has all the taste, man, for the fine things.

I feel that I can do anything. That's the way I am. I can do
everything at once. Or I can't do anything. I'm moving all the
time.

When you come here, you stagnate . . . you do nothing.
Nothing. I've seen it so often. It's terrible. People with good
minds . . . they just sit here and they can't remember and . . .
blah! Nothing. Pass the chillum. I've seen it in myself, you
know. And that's why I am anxious to get out. Maybe Western
society isn't so good, but, you know, it takes up your time.
That's important. Technology and capitalism is an excuse . . .
it's like in lieu of religion. Like I don't need religion any more,
because I have a drive and a need and a purpose in life. I might
change. I might make ten million dollars and decide this is
nowhere, man. I'll just put it in the bank and leave and that's it.
Forget it. Right now, that's where I'm at.

I plan to beat the system. That's how I got through college.
And I can beat it again. When I'm working on a project, man,
I'm working twenty-four hours a day and at night I'm thinking
about it. I always have this argument with my mother. She says
you gotta go to work, you gotta do stuff. I say I don't have to do
anything. I just have to have other people do something. I just
have to organize. I'm good at doing it.

Listen: I'll give you my final statement.

In Afghanistan they have a sport called Bozkashi. It's played

on maybe three football fields. But there are really no boundaries. And maybe a hundred horses. And there are supposed to
be different teams. But you really can't decipher them. They
take a goat and they cut its head off, and the object is to take the
goat and run. And that's what life is all about. To run. Take the
goat and run. And there's no boundaries. And no rules. And it
occurs every minute of every day. And it covers everything you
do. That's it.

In spite of his father's religious background, in spite of four
years of college, in spite of advantages which few people have,
Barry saw no essential meaning to human existence. Where
were his values? Barry's basic commitment was to no one but
himself. And the idea that there might be a deeper meaning to
human existence that would enrich his life was alien to him. The
center of his universe was power and money.

How many more are there like him? Barry will find his meaning
in his millions. He'll tell you it was in his chromosomes all along.

14 Joe

". . . the same kind of high, just different intensities. It puts your brain on a pendulum, man . . . a cosmic pendulum."

Joe was twenty-four but he looked thirty. Tall, heavy-boned, bad complexion. Dirty clothes, long, straggly hair, a Fu Manchu moustache. He wore a leather vest with many pockets. They were the storehouse of his walking pharmacopia. He had morphine. He had cocaine. He had acid. He had hashish. A pocketful of pills. In the course of the evening we spent with Joe in Kabul, he shot morphine twice. He took five or six tabs of acid. He smoked four chillums of hashish.

I have been here since January. I don't have a passport or a visa. And no money. I haven't had any money since January, so I live at the hotel . . . on credit. Like I know these people and I would really like to pay them if I could. And I will . . . eventually.

I've got one telegram from my family in all the time that I've been here. The telegram was from my brother. He just wanted to know if I was still here, how long I would be here. Send him a carpet, you know. Well, I've been away from home for a long time. I left America in 1967, for the first time. Went to Germany. In the army for two and a half years. I went back home in '68 for one month. And after the army I went home for a month and a half. Then in June of '70 I left with money to go and buy a motorcycle and spend the summer in Europe. Trying to find a girl.

I had tried to go to junior college right after the army. I got out in December of '69; but I couldn't cope with it—I just wanted to get wasted. Wasted again. On dope.

But I've got an organizing mind and I get my information and my connections together pretty good. Try to stay a step ahead, you know. So I didn't get busted, but a lot of people did. And I would take dope to those people in jail, you know. Smuggle it in . . . things like that. But the army was a gas . . . it really was. Well, I went in in '67, in the reserves in Michigan. And went through the whole American trip for five months and then got sent to Munich. About three days after I got to my post I was smoking pot for the first time. Soldiers turned me on. It was a good time.

I got started on dope when I was twelve. Airplane glue. For about three years. It was good but it's damaging stuff, you know. Well, history goes back—when I was ten I got burned on my face . . . gasoline. I had second- and third-degree burns. So I was ten years old and really fucked up. A true inferiority complex. I had these scabs for a long time. So, two years after that happened, I went from grammar school to the junior high school. Met lots of new people. Some of these guys had been tripping since sixth grade. They turned me on. It was just wild. We didn't really care about damage. We read some things, you know. We did it mostly after school. We would go to somebody's house or to a big field down by the railroad tracks or into the woods. It was beautiful. Changes of perception. A lot like ether or nitrous oxide. All these things for me are the same kind of high. Just different intensities. It puts your brain on a pendulum, man . . . a cosmic pendulum.

It was a gas. But my father sort of fucked things up in a totalitarian way. He has a plastics factory. They make plastic molds. He also has an honorary position as Deputy Sheriff. In certain areas of Michigan you have got to get a sheriff elected like that. You know, status. He's got the I.D. card. He's got other things that are cool . . . in a way; he's got a flash attachment for his car—it's a big Mercury, you know —something I can't drive. And he's got a siren on his car. And he's got a police receiver in his car and in his bedroom. Yes, this is real. He's got a plastics factory and he's one-quarter policeman.

I saw *The Graduate*, you know. In the army getting ready to go home is similar to getting out of college. Like what are you going to do? And then this guy says "plastics." Well my father wanted me to become a police scientist. I told him I wasn't interested; I just split. He had tried to put me in a juvenile home a couple of times. I got seven minors for possession of alcoholic beverages. In Michigan. And that's what put me in the army. And he busted me once for carrying fake I.D. Took me into the station and all. . . .

Like I broke the law. I'll tell you—three years of glue in junior high school and three years of being drunk in high school. It was hard. And then I got into the army. And then just getting stoned while there. Like I really fought reality all that time. When I was in high school, I'd just get drunk or whatever. We would go to school at seven thirty in the morning, and we would stay in the parking lot and drink a few beers. Go to homeroom and sleep through most of school. It was a combination of good and bad years. But I even got kicked out my last month before finals . . . in '66. I was in school and the assistant principal kept hassling me in the hallways and calling my mother and shit like that. And finally it just came to a head and they gave me the boot. But I did have a good counselor . . . a woman. I had had her for three years. And she knew my history and she went and talked to the principal and he said, okay, I could graduate.

Graduation? I got drunk in the parking lot. My older brother had flunked one year, so he was graduating too. My father was there. My brother had gone to all the practices. But I just sat outside, heard my name on the p.a. system, and opened another bottle of beer. Sometime later I picked up my diploma for my folks' sake. But, you know, I didn't learn anything there. I learned a hell of a lot in the army. I went in when I was eighteen. I was a tanker. I took care of the tanks.

I joined the army instead of going to jail. Like I was in a courtroom. And I don't know what I am going to do. . . . I'm on probation from the same judge for two years for the sixth bust. And like I graduated from school, but I'm a bum, and he knows it. This is rich suburbia, you see, and this black guy gets up there for armed robbery and he gets up there and starts jive-talking and tells the judge that he's going to join the army and make a new man out of himself, serve his country, and all kinds of shit he was throwing at the judge. That was '66. This is all in the courtroom. So the bailiff stands up and reads out the charge and the judge says, "How do you plead?" And he says, "I plead guilty." And he says, "Do you have anything to say before I pass sentence?" You know, it's all formal. He put me in jail before, weekends, in the county jail. So when I got up there, the judge says the same thing to me, "How do you plead?" "Guilty!" "Do you have anything to say?" "I want to join the army, reform myself." Bang! twenty-five-dollar fine and the chance to split. I saw the black guy say it, so I said it. That's it. So, okay, I join the army.

I was afraid of jail; that was the big thing. I spent two weekends in the county jail and that was plenty. The jail was dirty and I was a seventeen-year-old kid. I mean, you know, guys in there want to get familiar . . . rape . . . robbery. From the looks of it, I had a twenty-year-old mattress. It was pretty fucked-up. It was just two weekends. I had been in the city jail before for other things. I spent a couple of nights there. But for the sixth bust, he said, "You go to school Monday through Friday, but Friday you come to the police station." Which I did . . . for two weekends in a row. At the big jail, that was where the sheriff's office was. And my father had been elected. And he had to come Sunday evenings and pick me up. He taught us to drink. We all had police records—all five of us. And my mother was always going to the jail to get somebody out.

It was the fact that my father was never home. He was always involved in business and if anything went wrong with the kids, then my mother was to blame. That's why she never told him. That's why she turned into an alcoholic. We were alcoholics, too. All of us. We had a big, big house. Lots of room. Always plenty of food. And it was a house, you know, security. But certain things . . . like clothes . . . they were cheap. He was really a miser in some ways. Like we never had an allowance, for instance. To get money, I had paper routes, dishwashing jobs, caddy, that type of thing. At four thirty in the morning, get up to deliver papers. Deliver papers for an hour and a half. Go back home, wash up, eat breakfast, go to school. And drink a couple of beers in the parking lot. School was, you know, cliquish . . . and scary.

I was with the same group through most of school. I got into a fraternity. That was wild, because they were illegal in Michigan. And if you get busted, you lose credits and all that shit. Yes, it was wild. We had the biggest parties. The wildest parties. The best parties. And the most people getting busted. Those were status symbols . . . trouble with the police.

Funny, but over here I am a vegetarian mostly. I eat eggs. LSD is, you know, the space age. The twentieth century. That's how I trip. But the other things are okay with me, too. Yes, the hash thing, oh, yes, in Germany. That's why we were down there . . . with three locked doors behind us. These guys would supply us. I was in Munich for the first fourteen months. Yes, so three days after I got to Germany, down in the basement, I was smoking hash. I got turned on. Hashish. Turkish. I got sick. Because I didn't smoke cigarettes. It was like tripping. Something good. A new thing. A lot of spades in the army. It was something you had to be committed to. You had to want to get stoned. And we were constantly stoned. That was the big thing. There was a cat there who was always trying to bust us. It was weird; he could tell who was turning on. Well, there were formations and everybody straight—except the few people you knew. You didn't mind things then because you were smoking dope. And you were paranoid, because you could have been busted. But it . . . it was . . . a war.

So I was in Germany in the army. I was in the army environment in a foreign country. Tried to get wasted because reality was totally fucked.

I finally got discharged from the army. It was a gas. But it got to be a time of real paranoia. I had a friend—he shot himself in the mouth with a 45. It was real heavy. Chaos.

After the army, I went home with eighty-five grams of good Pakistani in my pocket. Twenty-six cigarettes—German cigarettes—that were filled with this really good hashish. I flew from Frankfurt. And the stewardesses . . . they were, like, beautiful. And I was smoking and smoking. And I was getting so stoned. And the lights came on for take-off. Okay, I had all this dope and I had to go through customs in a few hours. And like I really wanted to take the dope through customs because it was such a game. Sure, it was good dope, but it was more for that reason. I had it right there in a plastic bag . . . in my nicely pressed green uniform. And I just grooved on it, you know. Anyway, I just walked off that plane and teetered up the hallway. And these two stewardesses were standing right there. It was like a commercial.

So I was going through customs. And everyone said, "Hi, G.I." It's a trip. They found a bottle of Librium—which is connections again. People in dispensaries. Just go in and open the door and take what you need. One guy freaked out about it. The other guy joked about it. He was getting out of the army. And like he'd been *in* the army and he *needed* the Librium. And I told them I had all these things that you aren't supposed to bring back . . . your canteen and stuff. The shit you live with. It's recycled. G.I. Government-issued. 1944. My army field jacket. So I had to stay at Fort Dix a night or two for processing. I got up in the morning with my dope in my pocket. Went through these different orientations. G.I. Bill, the insurance, that stuff. It was pretty cool.

I kept on finding myself doing these completely outrageous things . . . but it was all part of keeping my head in the game. So, between the orientations, I smoked my joints and an officer would walk by and I'd say, "Fuck you" . . . real fast. And he'd say, "What'd you say? What, what?" I gave them my papers finally, which had been all doctored, and they gave me four hundred dollars. And they handed me my discharge papers. They took me to the airport. And after I got on the plane I went into the john and took all this stuff . . . dogtags, my shirt . . . and I stuffed them down the john. By the time I got home I could hardly stand up . . . really stoned.

It was about nine o'clock at night when I arrived. Well, it was pretty bad right from the beginning. Like my father was pretty freaked out about all the other trips that were going on with youths. Like he's got four sons and six weeks later he kicked them all out of the house. When I came home from the army he just refused to communicate with me. It was worse than if we were strangers. And I gave him this shit, you know. I just told him where he stood. Told him he was fucked up. I had just never stood up to him. Never. I mean that was the trip before. We never got it back together. We still haven't. I just split . . . about a week later.

My mother was the go-between. She kept secrets. She tried to keep the old man mellow. But . . . I don't know these people, man. I just don't remember them. I can't even remember their faces. I don't know those people anymore. I mean it's a shock to see how they are. Just over the years. I see my older brother —he's married, got two kids, he works for the old man. The next brother under him—he's like twenty-four now—he holds the record for ego for my family. He's always coming to me and saying, take it easy on the old man. It's too much for him. He still doesn't understand.

But I went home anyway, because I had thought about school. So I went home and I enlisted—that's how it turned out—I enlisted in a junior college. I remember taking a course in introductory psychology. And a reading course, because I was so totally away from reading. I only had to be there like six hours a week. Because for me, I read slowly. But I drank and smoked dope. I also got into peyote capsules.

Later, I went back to my girl friend in Germany.

When I returned to Germany I went to her apartment and she wasn't home. I was waiting, I remember. I am with her brother and I am waiting for her to come in. I really wanted to be with her . . . I really felt that she was the only person I could communicate with. I loved the chick, that was it. And, you know, it was just great to be with her. But . . . you know, I was a G.I. and running away from my environment. So these trips came down heavy.

There was another guy; she didn't know that I had flown back. She didn't expect to see me for a while. We had been writing letters—but then I just split and came back. And so like she comes back with this other guy and we go upstairs and I had dope and we started smoking. And we talked and talked. The three of us. I was just really blown out, you know. And I loved this chick. And I came back to her to be rescued. Finally, I just swallowed my last hopes, my pride—everything. All my earthly belongings. At that exact moment, I couldn't even cry. I just didn't know what was going on. I wanted to cry, but I couldn't cry; I just didn't know what was going on. Imagine, I couldn't even get it together enough to cry. It came down to two things—make it better or finish it.

I went and checked into a hotel, took a shower and changed, took some of this peyote that I had and laid back and thought about everything. And during this trip I changed a lot of things. I stopped smoking cigarettes. I became a vegetarian. Stopped biting my fingernails. And just tried to bring order to the chaos. Under the influence of the dope. It wasn't too strong a dose—it was just one big cap of peyote. Not even especially hallucinatory. But I brought out certain things. Saw the light. Saw the connection to earth again. I saw "connections." The light and the electric wire and it went into the wall and it was connected to something else and behind it all was this energy source. I saw this light as my life. Organic, living. My life was simply a case of the switch being off. And how do you turn it back on. This chick . . . she triggered it. She brought it all down . . . the chaos.

She came to the hotel later. It was getting dark when she came. It was February and about five-thirty. It had been all those hours that I had been thinking about things. Then she came and we just talked. But we weren't really back together. Anyway, the whole thing ended up a trio; that was really heavy. You know, me, this guy, and this girl.

It flipped me out. I tried to be easy with everybody. I knew her feelings about this guy. I knew he was fucked up—and that she would come to realize that. I'm a tripper. I knew her. And with this guy she just had an infatuation of some sort. And a lot of the time I just walked away from them. It lasted about two months. Six weeks it was kinda on and off . . . together. And then for a while she was actually living with me at my place.

But the big thing was a trip we took about two days before I split. We had gotten some blotter acid; it was very good. You know, there are times when you feel that you shouldn't take LSD. We didn't know, but we were going to do it together, right. So we took the acid and we went into this park in the middle of Munich and we're going around there and we had this tab of mescaline, so we took that as well. Later in the night, after a lot of things had gone on—weird things—we ended up in this guy's flat, the other guy's flat. He was out of town or something. But this is on a trip, you see, and we're in this guy's flat. For us now, we're on one and a half trips. All I can say is that we really got it together. We just came together again and we knew it was cool. Then I had to split two days later.

I had to go home and start a lawsuit for a motorcycle accident that I had had in '66. To see people. To see whatever was going on at that time. I don't know. Anyway, I went home for a month and a half and I got eighteen hundred bucks cash. I had two grams of Thailand junk that I smuggled home. Pure, ninety-six percent, pure junk. And, man, I was just cruising. And I split. Detroit airport. Eighteen hundred bucks in my pocket.

Economy class ticket—$280. Some guy came up—he had on a business suit—and he sat next to me. So he said to me, "You've got a one-way ticket . . . why?" And I said, "Well, I don't know if I'm coming back." And then he said, "Well, how much money do you have?" I guess he was concerned about my welfare or something—more than I was. I was leaving those bastards behind.

And like all this time I was snorting this junk. And later I was driving and I could only like do fifty miles per hour because I was so strung out. Just driving all day and night. Over five hundred miles. Snorting this junk. Junk is really a pain-killer, you know. But it was good . . . a groovy way to drive. But I overdosed kinda. So I had to park and I fell out and woke up with two German policemen standing over me. And they were just looking at me. But it was cool. And I got on my way again. Driving all night. Snorting some junk. You know, nodding out in the right lane . . . waking up in the left lane. I did that at least ten times. Honest. So I finally got in about ten at night and I went straight to her place; but she wasn't home . . . she had hitchhiked away. Again with this other dude—but only because he was fucking her. And they had gone down to southern France to join these gypsies. I forget the name of the place. And then she finally split the dude and went to Egypt. On her own. So I ran down to Greece and jumped on a boat.

And I finally caught up to her and took her back across the English Channel, took her back, smoking dope all the time. We camped a few days outside of London and she split the airport and that's really heavy. But we really had a good summer together. And then I just went out, jumped on my bike and headed back to Munich and the chick was doing other things.

We were kind of far apart then, both going in strange directions. And being with other people . . . not jealousy, but controlled jealousy . . . you know, kinda let it burn. And then she died last July. I came back to Amsterdam last December. In December we got it back together. Then we were living together . . . and then we got into fixing. Experimenting with fixing. And then, we did a lot of other things . . . cooked a lot of hash cakes, and that kind of thing. And then lived in Munich for a while. Then we split for India . . . May 7, 1971. We were in India for fourteen months. In India it wasn't contacts at all. I was fixing. I was totally in another world and I had premonitions. Doing a few tricky things . . . like altering papers and stuff. But finally I got situated in a hotel where the people were just easy. People at the same time were getting thrown in jail and they were being bussed back to the hotel. Yeah, I went first to the income tax people . . . went through a thing with them. Like . . . my chick was down and she died. She was nine days in the hospital. It was very unsettled. It was very complex—physically, she had been weakened for a long time. And then, she had hepatitis in February and we cleared that. She had had the problem of intestinal virus too long—and a lot of weird trips came down to emergency. Had to have an emergency appendectomy in the best hospital in Bombay . . . and the surgeon came out of the operating room and told me . . . she was dead.

Then I split Bombay and took my last shot—she had been cremated. All sorts of things had to be done. Her ashes had to be sent to the United States. My parents had telexed. . . . I had gone to TWA and I sent a telex message to Detroit, and then to suburbia. It came back with a ticket and $150 spending money. A ticket to Munich. It was a turmoil for me going back to be with her family. It was just heavy. Her father had died in '67. Then, I felt responsibilities. I took this chick away from her home. But her family didn't hate me. Compassion on both sides. But after a while there were certain sentiments. Things her brother would say.

I tried to stop fixing. I was on methadone for five days . . . and I went cold turkey completely for five days. Then I was taking some dex's. But it was a physical trip. It was total physical . . . I wasn't trying to escape. My body was just trying.

Even with the chick . . . we lost interest in sex. It's masochistic. You know you're killing yourself in a certain way. You get into it. It's such an involvement. But they say it's a sexual thing. The needle is a huge sexual. I mean like, okay, if you're with some people and you subconsciously play a role and you take something to be heavy, that's one thing. But when you're by yourself and you're heavy . . . you whip off your belt and you tie it off really heavy and it's your life if you can really keep a steady supply. It's running away. Okay. The girl is dead. My life is shattered. I'm hooked on morphine. Physically I don't want it. I hate it. I'm a slave. I'm trying to fight it. A few times I just threw it away. I broke my syringe with the butt of a rifle. My friends tried to help me. Then I've gone back on it. Just a physical dose. I got back and I got back into it. In New Delhi I was buying and selling. . . . I took drugs because it opened doors. I know myself when I'm not stoned and that very often I'm not natural man in twentieth century, steel and concrete and iron and I don't feel nature except under the influence of these kinds of drugs. And I want to feel nature. I know that's where I belong.

Joe's hold on reality was tenuous. He was compulsive about tying everything he told us to a specific date. He was compulsive about his drug paraphernalia. Every time he smoked a chillum he reached into his pocket, took out a small flannel bag, untied the strings, and took out a handkerchief-wrapped chillum. Out of another pocket would come another little bag filled with hashish. He removed the hashish, broke off a piece, balled it in his hand, and then carefully pressed it out like a pancake. He rolled the pancake back into a ball and put it into the top of the chillum. He then put the hashish back in his pocket and smoked.

When he finished the chillum, he took the handkerchief and carefully drew it through the chillum to clean it. He then spread the handkerchief out flat, laid the chillum carefully on it, neatly rolled it up, inserted the wrapped chillum into the bag, tied the strings, and back into the pocket it went. Joe was orderly in his insanity. We got the feeling that if he ever broke the order it wasn't the chillum that would break—it was Joe.

Now I don't do anything outrageous except smoke hashish.

I'm not a smuggler. But I've got to live. I'll stay until they throw me out. I'd feel much easier about having a visa, and some money. I'm looking for three hundred dollars right now and recommunication with my brother.

On Saturday we visited some Americans who were in jail. I couldn't think of anything worse to describe what I saw. They don't feed you. I mean you're on your own as far as getting any food. The flies that were in the yard . . . they said they were two hundred times thicker in the cells. I've heard a lot of stories from a lot of friends who have been there. If they're going to bust me . . . I mean it gets into an aesthetic thing. I mean, I'm into mind inspiration with the use of drugs. And I honestly think that turning on to things like hashish makes you aware.

But smoking cigarettes is destructive. What I'd like to do is to start limiting my use. Because the body can reject. You don't live in Detroit so you've got fairly clean air . . . and your body can do it. But I overdose. But I've got to take acid. I've got worms. It's weird. I take acid and eject the worms. That's happened two times. I've gone to the toilet and there were the worms. I've seen them before sometimes . . . I mean like totally. Like if I eat a big dose of garlic and go to the toilet. It happened today.

In a lot of ways I think the world is fucked. And I think dangerous. The whole world's strung out. Ninety-nine percent of the people are either drugged out on diets or doped out on alcohol. Everybody's abnormal. It's a really fucked-up world. And they're too many people in power who can really play games with themselves. I have my good times, but there's times when I'm scared. I've got to start to see good things in myself.

I have just started to feel really at peace with myself. Coming to Afghanistan I had to do certain things. You find inner courage. Smoking hashish and doing LSD are not escapes. Not escapes.

The big thing in my life is not to escape but to be with a chick and spend time with the chick. Get into it. Two people together as being one.

Joe's father was a Deputy Sheriff. Joe's father was a rich, successful plastic mold manufacturer. Joe's father ruled his family with an iron fist. Joe's mother couldn't handle it; she was an alcoholic. Joe couldn't handle it either. He was the son of his father but he didn't want to be his father's son. So at the age of ten he subconsciously set out to break himself. He succeeded.

15 Mrs. Coufal

"I think parenthood should be an honored profession, and that people who do not accept that honor make a terrible mistake."

Mrs. Coufal is in her early thirties. Her husband is a highly successful lawyer in his forties. They have three children who range in age from five to eleven. Their son Jack, their eldest, is adopted.

Over the past several years, the guest room of their city apartment has been occupied by a young relative. They have had nieces and sisters as house guests. In their church and political work, they have frequently associated with young people. We felt it would be a good idea to interview a couple who had been involved with people in that age group to see if that association had had any impact on their attitudes toward raising their own children.

I did want to live in the city because I thought here we would have much more to do with our children until they were much, much older and that would seem natural. Whereas if we lived in a suburb, at a very early age they would be off and away from us. I want to be involved with them constantly . . . every move they make, every person they know, everything they do. Thus our reason for living in the city. And the choice of schools. The schools they go to stop at the eighth grade, partly with the thought that that insulates them from older children who would be involved with drugs. We understand that drugs are prevalent in all the lives of young people. Children of friends. Relatives. It think it's just awful. Eighth-graders smoking marijuana. But I'm always with my children. I go everywhere they go and I do everything with them. So it's going to be very difficult for them to get into drugs with me around. I guess it will have to happen in the school. I would worry because I don't think the schools take a strong enough stand on that . . . well, on everything.

I mean, kids who were smoking in eighth grade at Jack's school were sent home for two weeks. Well, I think they should be sent home forever. I think the school should have certain codes . . . for drinking, or leaving the school building. They would just have certain rules and the kids would know ahead of time that if they broke those rules, that's the end of their time at that school. And it should be so clear to the kids that it inhibits them. Sexual intercourse in high school doesn't bother me quite as much, depending on the atmosphere in which they were having intercourse . . . not in Volkswagens! But I feel strongly about marijuana used during those years. There are too many things for kids to handle. And I think that the private schools, in fact the society, simply do not have the measure of social cohesion, social intimacy, and social structure that makes it possible for everyone to get his head together on these questions. To decide on standards which are then carried out.

That's what bothers me very much about the schools that our children go to; namely, there is no community. There is no group of parents that know each other well enough and interact enough so that they can get together on their ideas. Instead, the name of the game is diversity, individualism. You know, it's fine politically. But it's an idea which may be displaced, and misplaced, in terms of values in raising children.

Well, we initiated conversations when Jack came home with a story about marijuana. He was quite shocked, so I drummed in on that shock. You know, what a terrible thing, the kids messing themselves up that way. Another time, we were pouring a glass of wine, and Jack said, "I'd like some of that." We said that it wouldn't be a good idea. You have enough trouble growing up, and you have to concentrate on that. It's only by the time you grow up and really work out a lot of things for yourself that you'll be ready to drink a little bit.

My feeling is, if only they didn't have to go to school at all, they would be further ahead. When I send them off in the morning, I think, "Well, they're going to have some interesting experiences." I really feel I've watered down my clout by separating them from us, and I really sound like a—a blanket! But I don't think they're smothered like that. I think they're very independent. In most things they are.

If they didn't go to school, I would raise them the way I'm raising them now, except that they would be removed from those particular influences. You know, from people who don't know how they feel about children smoking marijuana, for instance. When I went to boarding school, there wasn't any question about it. I mean, no headmaster was confused. He knew. You smoked, you left. Finished. And I don't understand why in such a short time, twelve or fifteen years later, the headmaster is confused. I don't understand. The point is, if he's confused on this issue, he's confused on every issue. There is no sense of any standards, in virtually any regard. Sometimes we feel that we would like very much to start our own private school, or *I* would, where we would select parents who shared the ideas that we have . . .

We have about five possible candidates! If that many. But the point is that then you would have parents who share the same point of view on some of the important questions. It isn't just sex and drugs, but it's also a question of other important values that schools don't recognize. Such as belief in God. Even interest in it.

Barbara goes to Bible class, a midweek Bible class. I thought it would bolster her, I mean I thought it would be nice if she went there with a classmate, and I tried to find a classmate to go with her. Well, the most likely candidate turned me down with, "We are not Bible-y." There it is. There isn't anyone who is even mildly interested in their children being exposed to religious questions. If the school just had a course in the history of religion or something, but nothing, nothing. Not mentioned. I mean, *not mentioned*. Like a whole area of human life never happened. I mean, it's like ignoring the astronauts or something.

I'm not personally interested in getting involved in drugs, something that might unhinge me. I mean, I'm very pleased now with my personality, and handling things, and I don't want to fool with that. Even in drinking, I really don't drink more than a little wine any more. Things are nice the way I am. I think that getting involved with any kind of drugs or liquor kind of messes you up.

I would think that part of the reason kids do smoke marijuana is to experiment. But they also do it to avoid situations that may be frightening to them: school work, or other kinds of work, relationships with people that are difficult. You know, they're just kind of off from that, they don't have to experience relationships with people, because they're kind of in a fog, you know, whatever the feeling is from smoking. I've heard psychiatrists say that the challenges of growing up, sexual maturity, for instance, is enormously detoured. They go into that world and their sexual development is just not dealt with. They don't face the challenge of a social situation without stimulants.

The whole sexual thing, for example. I think that probably even fifteen years ago it wasn't that important to a lot of young people. Now there's a destruction of values. No self-structure. No discipline.

If one of my daughters is fourteen, sixteen, eighteen and involved with a boy, "Do I recognize where they're at . . ." Yes, I'll probably get an impression of what their relationship is. And I think I have a standard which would make me either pleased with it or very displeased with it. A lot would depend, first of all, on how she was functioning in the rest of her life; if she was still good in school, as she is now.

If she's "lousy" in school, well, I'd be worried about that then. It wouldn't be just the fact that she was sleeping with some boy.

School is a big activity for sixteen years old. If that fails her, then that's the big problem.

But if she likes to dance, and she's a great dancer, and that's what she's been doing for six years, that's terrific. I love that. I wouldn't accept "contemplation." I'm not convinced that she's a really great contemplater. I guess I'm more of an active person and if she was a great horseback rider, terrific. If she was marvelous with children and she really wanted to spend most of her free time babysitting and working in Sunday schools and doing things like that, I'm all for it. You know, so she's getting C's in school. She can struggle along for a while; then not go on to school. I mean, I'm not very big on higher education. A child would have to show me first that they were really interested in college before I'd be interested in having them go to college. I don't see that as the only route. It's just that when they're sixteen, I think they've got to be concentrating on what they are aside from their sexual activity. And if their sexual activities are predominant, I would feel that we'd gone wrong somewhere a long time ago. You can't start saying when they're sixteen, "Gee, you should feel differently about yourself." All the qualities that would make them a certain way are reinforced all along the way. A year ago I would have denied the possibility of my not knowing everything about my daughter and her friends. But I now recognize that it's possible. Already we feel that we know less than we want to know.

That's another problem, you see, that has to do again basically with how the schools are structured. No one knows what goes on in the school. I don't think teachers know. That's a terrible thing. Children's lives become very fragmented because of this. This is part of the social fallout.

There's also a tremendous emphasis on diversity, on "do your own thing."

A couple of weekends ago, Jack had a friend up. And Jack's behavior was antisocial. He wasn't doing his own jobs, which were very modest—his chores; and he was really getting sassy. It was very hard to deal with that problem, because he had someone with him. And we didn't do the hard thing; we waited until we got back to the city and his friend had been taken home and then we had an explosion. Which was a very, very bad way of handling it. It should have been handled Friday night, when the storm signals were up.

I want to say something else, that at sixteen I had a very good sense of what my parents expected, what my parents thought about certain ways of behaving. And I would assume that our children would have that same feeling.

I think the question of sexual activity of older teen-agers is a hard one for me, and maybe my ambivalence will make it harder for my children. I think if a fifteen-year-old girl was involved with sex promiscuously it would say something so terrible about the way she felt about herself that I would really feel we had a terrible problem on our hands, and she had a terrible problem.

Our whole thing is being parents. I mean, it's so important to us, and we just like it so much. We also feel we're very good at it. It's our major interest. Some parents are saying, well, do your own thing. Everything has changed about the views of family. I mean there's such a difference in the attitude about marriage and about child rearing and about family. And so we all face kind of a problem about how to interpret these changes and values to our children. I think the only salvation, the only hope I have is if you keep close to them somehow. Even when they're ready for college I would say go to a day college—the way colleges are now—and live at home. And we'll keep slinging it back and forth, so they at least have the impact of our feelings and thinking about things; they don't get thrown off from us for three months, surrounded by completely unsure, undecided adults on all these questions, and these peers whose values keep changing. You would hope that if you sent them to boarding school, they would get that from the faculty, but I know now that they would not. So all you can hope is to keep them around as much as possible, to keep pumping it in. But times being what they are, you don't know what's going to come out.

I mean, elementary school obviously has its problems. A simple thing, like there was candy on Barbara's school bus. Kids were bringing it. So I called up the director of the lower school and said, "Don't you think you could send a letter home?" just assuming that she would agree with me that candy first thing in the morning is not a great way to start the day. Well, no—there's a different point of view on that. But more than that—"We have so many rules," she said. "We wouldn't want to make another rule."

I think people have a misguided idea about what freedom is, and what self-expression is. We have the idea that we're sort of amoebic! If anything were to press down on us in any way, or to form us in any way, we would somehow have lost something. When in fact I think we would have gained everything.

So many young people are lost. They're just finding their own way. Wanderers on the face of the earth. Well, you found them in Afghanistan. I don't know what made them start to wander, but it's really epidemic now, it seems, compared to twenty years ago.

I think it's shameful that that's the case, because it seems to me it's such a waste. There are lots of things to do, and there are lots of things that need being done. I mean there is so much to learn that I just can't see a kid being in college saying, "There's nothing to do here." That's terrible. That's a terrible indictment of the student and the college.

Maybe one of the problems about sex, or the lack of sex in the "old days" when it was forbidden, was that the result was there was an enormous amount of sublimation, which was supposed to enhance an adolescent's activity in other areas. Now, we don't build in the sublimation. You know, they're already gratified sexually, so there's no sublimation, so there's no drive in other areas. I mean, maybe that's what's happened.

I think parenthood should be an honored profession, and that people who do not accept that honor make a terrible mistake. Being a parent is one of the most important things one can ever do, and it's one of the hardest. I do think that people haven't concentrated on it; it's not been the center of their lives.

But I haven't lost. I feel very confident that with a lot of effort, you can make a difference. That is, you can pretty much succeed in either excluding or attenuating these negative outside influences. For example, we don't have a television set. That in itself produces more family interaction. The children are relating to each other and to us, because they're not sitting there in front of the tube.

Maybe television was the immediate straw that broke the camel's back, the cause of what's happened. That is the new factor. And all of that started, really, in the forties. And it took eighteen years to have its impact. Television is fine for adults. But it interrupts the maturational process, the growing-up process.

I just think for the parents, all they can do is keep slugging at it. . . . Spend a lot of time on their children. And I hope my children do something that has to do with somehow caring about other people; that whatever they pursue is not simply a kind of activity or work that is only for themselves.

I would like them to be Christians, yes. I sort of think they will be; I just take it for granted that they will be.

I want them to be effective—being effective in the sense of being able to do a job and stick to it and be parents and be responsible for their children, take care of their children. You know, meet life in a direct way and contend with it and make the best of certain experiences. In terms of talent, in terms of caring for people around them and their families. . . . That's what I hope we all are trying to do. That's what it's all about.

I also hope that we're all very close to each other, all through it. I hope that we're very close to them when they're adults, and that we are involved in their lives and they in ours, all the way. I would just as soon they didn't live in Nevada, but I could live with that.

Another thing—I would not want them to be big consumers. I think that's really bad . . . you know, a car, and spending a lot of money on clothes, and travel, food and restaurants, I just wouldn't want them to do that.

Since the Coufal children are not grown yet, it is difficult to determine whether or not their parents' attitudes will make a constructive difference in their development. You might not agree with some of Mrs. Coufal's premises or arguments about child-rearing, but you cannot argue with her sincerity.

As we talked to the Coufals, we recalled how many youngsters talked about a "childhood without parents." For the Coufal family, this would not be true. Truly, for them, parenthood has been an honored profession.

16 Donna

"Sometimes I stand in the way of my own freedom."

A bright sunny morning. A small mousey-looking girl stood in a courtyard with an armful of wet wash. We watched as she walked across the yard. She carefully hung her wash on a dirty old rope strung along a wall.

"Oh, hi, I forgot you were coming. Sometimes I really can't handle the dirt. The hotel manager heated some water for me. I was finally able to wash some of my things and Bill's too."

When she was done, we sat down in the shade.

I didn't have this place in mind as a special place to come to this summer. Bill was coming to the East again and invited me to come along. I had a little bit of money that I had saved while I was working back home, so I figured what the hell! Spend the money now because if I didn't I'd probably spend the money on school next year anyway. And I know I'll get by in Kabul on the

159

money I have. Even if you had much money there's not much to buy. It's cheap here. Nobody cares half the time . . . the toilet, the filth, much less the smell. The toilet is filthy. Someone else has shit on top of someone else's shit. Try and clean that up.

I have absolutely no right to harp on somebody else . . . People are here a couple of days or a month. It doesn't infringe on my freedom. Infringing on my freedom is if someone was doing something outright to hurt me or to take something from me or my loved ones. Then I'd do something. But it depends on what it would be, I guess. I yell but it's just not good. Sometimes I stand in the way of my own freedom.

If I came here again I wouldn't stay so long. Once I was here I would take trips. Maybe a trip to Bamiyan or a trip to Mazar-i-Sharif and I'd break it up so that it wasn't one month here in this hotel even though this hotel is fine . . . good. There are nice people around. I haven't found any hotels with good people and clean toilets. I've made my trade-off.

I have bad bug bites all the time. There's not much to do about them. You put some salve on and then you sweat so that ten minutes later any salve you put on is gone. I have dysentery. Four friends that had been in the East told me that . . . you know . . . you come to Afghanistan and you're going to get dysentery. You can take some pills. They'll make you feel better for a couple of days, but then it'll come back after that. I took Mexiform, which started to work for a couple of days when we were traveling. But then the dysentery started again, so I stopped taking pills. I got dysentery a couple of times . . . once pretty badly. I think it was strong . . . high fever . . . and I had it and Bill had it. Then Dan had it, then our friend Tom had it. Same symptoms. I think it might be nice, though, to take pills for everything that bothers you. But I haven't had it for over four days. Before we start back I plan to get Tetracycline or Mexiform. Here I'm pretty comfortable. I don't have to go anywhere at any time of day. I have no restrictions whatsoever. So I can, you know, wander around. If I'm not feeling too well with the dysentery I can just sit right in my room, and walk right across the hall to the toilet. If I did it over again, I would plan to bring medicine.

That kid that's sitting over there on the green has amoebic dysentery. He almost passed out when we were downtown once. Some Christian kids came around here and brought him back to their house and nourished him back to health. That not eating right is really stupid. A lot of the kids come here to be irresponsible. Just to really . . . fuck off. And, they don't really care one way or the other too much. They don't want to care . . . they're sick . . . they're stoned most of the time so it doesn't matter that much. Other things matter more than the dysentery. They probably don't think that they're not getting any nourishment.

I don't know. I can't see taking money from home to come on a trip like this and then just fall apart someplace, and then go back to become renourished and revitalized by mommy and daddy. And then come back and play again. That's no good. That's a worthless way of living. Not too many that I've met are into that. I don't think in this hotel anyway. These are the people I've been together with all the time.

You know the Peace Hotel, right next door? You'll find those kids over there at that hotel are on a heroin-morphine trip. Most everybody here has done that trip on their own and has done it for maybe a better reason than just to have your hit of morphine. You see a bit more aggression with the German kids. . . . I think they're maybe more polite with one another, but if something's wrong, they'll be the first to say something. French kids seem to hassle a lot; if the slightest thing is wrong, they yell about it. The Americans are usually . . . pretty American. Used to more comforts than a lot of other kids. They're always expecting more; they seem more comfortable. Like this place is nice compared to a lot of other hotels. It costs about twenty-five or thirty-five cents a night. The others cost about the same, but aren't as nice. At least the ones I've been in. You do have to brush the flies off yourself but there are flowers here and there's a jar of water over there that's cool all the time. There's a good management that's willing to build a fire in the bathroom for a hot shower when you want it. You get your tea within fifteen minutes most of the time. It's a good hotel.

When I go back home to the United States, I'll be going to school upstate New York. I don't know what to major in. General studies, maybe. I'm interested in anthropology. I'll resume my studies but I'll take back having new experiences; of seeing Kabul, ancient and modern together. The impact of the modern on the ancient . . . the way the people here have had to adjust. You look at the people in Iran and the people in Kabul and they're not the same. The people in Iran haven't been as pressured with the conflicts of society like the people in Kabul. They've had pressure here in Kabul, I think, so they pressure back. The kids on the street say, "Bakshesh, bakshesh," [bribe money or a "tip"] and they follow you down the street. And yet the people—the shopkeepers—pull you into the store, literally pull you into the store. They bargain with you saying, "Just look and no buy." And then if you don't buy, boy, are they ever pissed off. People in Herat aren't like that, you know. Every customer comes in, it's okay, you look, you buy, you talk. Here it's, "Buy . . . why don't you want to buy this? Not cheap enough, I'll come down a little bit. You rich American." I'm not a rich American, but I suppose I'm very rich as far as they're concerned.

In the back of my mind I'll remember these people. I'll remember the train . . . four days, four nights . . . how twenty different powers came together with different needs and how everybody were strangers, except a couple of pairs of people who were friends. By the time the four-day train ride was over everybody in every car knew each other. It's been really great to walk down the streets here and see somebody we met in Meshed or Tehran. Somebody that we haven't seen since the train from Venice, and spend an evening with them. I'll remember all those things.

In my experience in the States, I just haven't found that kind of sharing we had on the train. When I go back, I don't think I'll find it there. I think you have to be in more of a situation where there's some hardship to have a community hold together like that. There's not much hardship in the States.

I don't know what will happen next year. I'm twenty-one now. I spent one year at one college where my sister went to school. I didn't like it there because I was living at home. You know, the problems at home. I was working too much and I knew it. And I knew if I was going to stay at home I was going to stay working there because I was making such good bread. I couldn't resist it. So I transferred myself. Didn't like it there either. So I didn't like two schools.

I do enjoy the association of young people. I don't especially like working. I think school is structured pretty nicely, so that there is a lot of freedom. If you want to get something out of it, you really can. I must admit that I haven't got as much out of it as I'd like to. I'm lazy. I put things off. Another day, another time. Things don't get done.

The town where I go to school now is good. I just love it. I live off campus with three other girls.

I lived at home in high school. That was a little bit rough. My parents were separated when I was fifteen, and it was not an easy separation. You know. Lots of lawyers and court and a lot of that kind of stuff. So that's why I was kinda happy to get away from home and them and go away to school. I needed a rest. At home there was a need for me to choose between my father and my mother. So I chose my mother. I am with her now. Not *with* her, but as far as loyalty goes, I am. I think I was always closer to her and it seemed that every time she needed someone to lean on, she kinda fell back on me. [We learned later, from one of Donna's friends, that her mother was an alcoholic.]

My father was out or away most of the time. He *said* he was at his meetings, but that doesn't sound so good to me. Oh, he was here and there with a few ladies a bit, you know. He was having some fun.

I had one older sister. She was away, she moved to Detroit when all this started going on. She got an apartment and got married two years after my parents separated. She was twenty-one.

I was basically on my own.

It's hard to say how long this whole business went on. But I kinda withdrew while it was happening. I was fifteen and I stayed home a lot and I worked. That's the way I saved up all this money. I worked all the time. It was just a couple of miles away. I took a bus. I was a waitress.

Oh, yes, I made a lot of bread. About $3.50 or $4.00 an hour. It varied a lot. Depended on what I was doing and what the weather was like. The job was in an ice-cream restaurant where they made their own ice cream downstairs. So if it was really cold out, there wasn't too much business.

Early high school was kinda miserable because I was so withdrawn. I didn't have any real friends. My sister was having an affair again and again. Most of the time I was pretty bottled up.

In high school a couple of friends I had known for a long time got into a sorority. So I became a member. Then I got to go to parties, you know, doing sorority things—football games, going to the canteen, cokes and ice cream.

I was only into drugs a little bit at this time. Maybe I smoked once a month. Go to a party and smoke. I was just smoking at first. Then I started tripping on acid. I didn't care for the sorority at all, not at all. Really pricky girls. Snobbish, into clothes, you know. It wasn't for me at all. So I started hanging around. And I saw other kids hanging around and they seemed a little bit cooler, so I thought I'd hang around them. We hung out at the cafeteria. At dances they would be a little bit away. Not up close. In corners. It was like they were having a really good time by themselves. So I started associating with them a little bit more and got into the hippy group at the high school. Then I got into the drugs a good bit more.

Well, at first, maybe I smoked every weekend. Then more and more over the weekends. Started tripping a lot. Maybe taking a little bit of speed. Then started to smoke every day. Then a little more tripping. Trying a few downs.

I got into dealing a little bit, too. I found most drugs were too expensive. Everybody I knew was dealing and said it was cheaper that way. You sell to your friends and your friends sell to you. I sold mostly hash. Easier I guess. Easier for me to cut it up into little pieces and sell that, instead of weighing this. Grass wasn't profitable. I eventually stopped dealing because I never made any money at all. I made what I smoked. That's about all. Smoking for free. Never could make any profit.

I went to Boston to see a few of my friends. We tripped. And it was just horrible. It wasn't so frightening as much as it was overwhelming. It was very unpleasant. I didn't feel at home with my friends. Not at all comfortable. I had been away from them. I couldn't seem to get anything together with them. So I thought: alone. Isolated.

The bad trip was basically a feeling of them and me. Their party. And I was totally on the outside. We were having a little party and someone said let's go down to my apartment. And it was a couple of friends that I had known. So we went to this guy's apartment. And I felt a little bit better alone with him. I started to trip heavy and I was alone with him and it was nice. We got along well together. But after that trip, I just don't think I wanted to play with anything like that again. It was just too much. I know that it was me but I was so alienated. They were saying come on, come on, come on. But I was really afraid that night. I don't know what I was afraid of. It was very difficult. I was at a loss for words. And when I wanted to say something it just didn't come out. So I just ended up being alone and by myself.

I was hundreds of miles into the universe.

I don't think I would take acid again. No, I just don't think so.

I really enjoyed the physical effects of drugs. It mentally defined things, too. Like every mescaline trip I took was a much freer thing than the acid. I was always out running around. Most mescaline trips were games really, out playing with people. But I wouldn't take it again because I don't feel like there is any need to.

Here I smoke probably every day. But to no extent really.

Probably less than a joint. Pass a joint around I might take a few tokes. Get stoned. I smoke ganga mostly. No, I don't smoke too much hash. I'd much rather do grass than hash. The hash is *so* strong. The grass is a little bit smoother. You can sit up and talk to guys rather than lay back in a chair.

I started getting interested in guys when I was about fifteen, and I reached a point when I started reaching out for something else. I never had too many boyfriends. I didn't feel like having a relationship with anybody else. I had a hard enough time dealing with myself then.

I was sleeping with just one boy at fifteen. He was about the same age. He worked at the same place I worked. And we saw each other at work and occasionally we would go to a dance together. And I slept with him but it meant nothing. I was like talked into it. I didn't particularly enjoy it because it wasn't my choice. I didn't really want it. I felt obliged.

I guess I was reaching out for somebody. And I didn't like the somebody I didn't reach. I guess I wanted to try it, too. But it was hard to tell him to fuck off. Maybe I gave him what he wanted, but I don't think so. I saw him for maybe three months.

Then after that I didn't have a steady boyfriend for at least a year.

We often had great difficulty hearing Donna. She spoke so softly that her voice was like a whisper. Occasionally tears would stream quietly down her cheeks.

I didn't have a steady boyfriend until my first year of college. I was really busy then with working and school. I saw him mostly weekends. Maybe once during the week we would go to a movie. I would sleep with him. I had a nice relationship with him, you know. It was nice because we shared.

I didn't want to start taking birth control pills then. I didn't see him enough. I wasn't close enough to him to do that. It was a nice relationship, but I didn't love him.

I shared things with my mother but not with my father. After about thirteen or so, I don't think I had anything in common with my father at all.

Oh, my father came in and had dinner and he was gone. I had no desire to speak to him. I could see that something terrible was happening to my mother. She was open and would talk to me and tell me, you know, a little bit. But not too much because I was too young, I guess. She didn't want to worry me. But I knew that something was wrong and that he was doing it. It never occurred to me to talk to my father. I really should have. It's a pity we don't speak to each other, especially now. I don't even see him anymore.

I know where he is though. He works at the same company he worked at before. I don't think it would be a good thing to contact him, especially insofar as my mother is concerned. She would feel betrayed. I don't think she's over it yet. She's very secluded in her house. About ten years ago she was in a car accident and she was crippled—partially crippled, anyway. So that threw her off. Then a few years after that my father started running around. So I don't think she's recovered from any of this.

She's about fifty-three maybe. Not so old.

Now that I'm not home very much anymore, she gets herself out. To the ladies auxiliary, you know. She has a couple of clubs, but not too active.

I had a car when I was in high school. I couldn't finish payments. I just left it at home. She took driving lessons. She learned how to drive. I thought that was okay. She almost lost her foot and she broke her neck in the car accident. She can't really turn her neck and she's got a really weak foot. And she's really paranoid in cars because of the accident. But she got in that car and she learned how to drive. I was pretty proud of that. I gave her lessons. I wasn't too patient with her. She would go so slow on the highways. I'd yell, "Faster, faster!"

When Donna yelled, "Faster, faster," we had the sense that it was one of the few times that she had truly asserted herself. Unlike the time when she found herself in bed with her boyfriend, this was a time when she was in control of the situation. This was a time that made demands on her. There was little in her background that had ever made her feel that she had rights or powers as an individual: the right to demand from her father that he be her father; the right to demand from her mother her own independence; the right to enjoy sex with her boyfriend; the power to create a life of her own for herself.

When Donna returns to the United States, will she ever get that feeling that she had on the four-day train ride?

"It's been really great to walk down the streets and see somebody we met. I'll remember all those things. I don't think I'll find it when I get back."

17 Robert

". . . everybody's trip is their own illusion."

It was eleven o'clock in the morning. We wandered into a courtyard restaurant. There was a young man sitting in the garden at a table. He was drinking a Coke and eating spaghetti. We sat down at another table and ordered.

We kept glancing over at him. His long dark hair hung down over his shoulders. He wore a native white pajama suit. His complexion was dark and his bold black moustache added vigor to his face. In spite of his Afghani dress, he was obviously an American.

"You guys American? Can I bum a cigarette?" We started to talk.

I've been here traveling as a tourist. I came here to see if I could do some importing and exporting but things didn't work out. A friend of mine got sick. He had to go back to the States.

169

And he abandoned me without any money. So I've been here for about eight months straight, without any money. I subsist through my friends, you know. You learn to talk to other people and they take care of you . . . straighten out visas, find doctors, buy you dinners, take care of your hotel bills.

I get along with people just the way I got along with my parents. My parents just have to understand, it's just another way of life. I haven't seen my father for ah, maybe ten years. It's lack of communication, separation. He doesn't want to be connected with me, at all. He's withdrawn because of my mother probably.

I was the youngest in the family. My father left when I was about eight, or we left my father . . . my mother just separated, because of alcohol. We moved to a different area of California altogether. My sister ran away from home and was put in an institution. She's okay now, she's living a really good life, and my brother quit high school at an early age and went in the air force. Then they put it on me to be the only one to graduate high school, which wasn't a very big thing to do. I did a little college, but because of my physical condition—I've got asthma—no one would take me on a job basis. I had a lot of police training, for example, before I found out I couldn't get into police work at all, government or otherwise.

I told my father about my problem but he just looked away from me. He's doing what he needs to do. I imagine he's still in construction work and living in Southern California. I think he's remarried—illegally. My dad is a draft dodger, and everything I think I've ever done in my life has been, in a way, against the structure. Like high school. I had a very strange high school. My mother, we lived five blocks from this high school, and my mother wouldn't send me there because she heard they smoked pot. So I had to go an hour and twenty minutes by bus to the other side of town to a high school that was much straighter. More money, you know, more money than I had, for sure. It was a hindrance because I was quite an athlete and I didn't get to partake in it. Also, I flunked history and English, just lost interest. Probably because I was separated from the people that I grew up with.

In my neighborhood, you could walk downtown and you could walk up to the hills. When you're a little kid growing up, I guess it makes quite a bit of difference. Yeah, it was good. I had a lot of religion thrown in then, too. . . . Yeah, I went to a religious high school; it was a Protestant high school that didn't let me partake in any public events of any type. Just straight religion. It was Pentecostal. It was restricting. At the age of eighteen, I just stopped.

My mother stressed working, so during high school I took some electronic courses, and that got me an instant job at an electronics company in about 1963, I guess. And I didn't adjust to that too good, factory working. It was a switch from high school, too much of a switch. I couldn't handle having money for one thing, because I never had any and all of a sudden I ended up with three or four hundred a month. It was bad, bad for me. I gave it to my mother. Working was something to do, but actually I wanted to go to school some more. Actually I wanted to go out and play in the world. In my last year in high school I cut classes all the time. The way I see it now, education is nowhere. Learning is nowhere.

Anyway, after I started working, I gave her money. Then I found I had some money saved and she said I could get a car. That changed things. I started going out in the world a little more. One job to another. Finally I got into auto parts. I worked in the same factory as my mother, as a matter of fact. That wasn't bad, but it was a waste of time as I see it now. It was just to work, at home, friends, drink, party, back to work, you know. Pretty regular.

Then I decided to become a policeman. It's in the family. My uncle was a chief of police in a city in California. But I didn't make the cops because of my asthma. That was a hard one. I started working again, and then I got into fencing. It was all by coincidence. I got into tripping behind LSD. The guy down the street who I grew up with happened to get into it before I did. He turned me on to LSD, not the right way. It wasn't good LSD. So through LSD and through smoking pot, you know, I met people who were into doing, say burglaries, for money. They were burglarizing places like industry. Or they would burglarize a bar. Uh, I never had the guts for a burglar. But I knew a lot of people because I lived in the neighborhood for a long time. That enabled me to be a fence for them.

The fencing was great, it was just fun, you know. I'd sell just to my friends. I'd sell televisions, stereos, tools . . . It wasn't a very big operation, that's the thing. It was very small.

Fencing lasted about six months. Yeah, I made about two thousand dollars in six months. On the last deal I was going to make three thousand dollars but it got busted. The deal got busted. It was a deal where they took some guns, it was right about 1968. Black Panthers were pretty heavy, Hell's Angels, all those things. And here's a party of poor burglars stealing two hundred guns, you know, not even connected with any of these groups. The cops really took out after us and we got caught. I was busted, too. But the California courts were really great. They found out it was a small thing; it wasn't a revolution or anything. The investigators were really nice people. I mean, the system's okay when you have to work within it. They worked within it, too. Protects you.

But the fencing was mostly all fun. It wasn't too much paranoia. The fun of people being able to get something at a lower price, because you know the factories are ripping us off anyway. One time they ripped off a whole drugstore. We were giving Mickey Mouse watches away. It took us three days to go through every drug. We didn't want to be selling ones we weren't supposed to. And we did find drugs in there that were very bad for you. There were warnings: "Five days until death." But it took us three days to go through two mailsacks full of drugs, separate the uppers and the downers and the stomach pacifiers. And then we sold or traded them for pot. The people that I was into weren't too much interested in reds or yellows, downers. Too dangerous.

I got married in there, too, to keep out of the law. I was

working at the same time. I met this chick about the same time I was fencing. She was having security problems in her head. She knew too much about my fencing and she had talked to the police a little too much. So I decided to get married so she couldn't testify in court against me.

We got the marriage certificate, we went through that. We got married the night before she was to talk to the police, but I ended up with the papers, which never got sent to City Hall. So she truthfully told the police that we were married, and they believed us, and they stopped the hassle. We separated right after that. She went back to Washington.

After that, I'd kinda had it, you know. I put on the brakes and slowed down, went back to just regular working and partying. Then I decided I needed to go to the mountains for a while, so I took off. I packed my stuff, got into my car, and took off for the mountains. It was beautiful in those mountains. I pitched my tent, unpacked my gear, and was completely alone. I loved it. I'd sit in the doorway to my tent, smoking a joint, looking out over the valleys to the sea and for the first time in my life I felt nice and quiet on the inside.

Since I had several pounds of pot with me, I had a lot of seeds. I had been saving seeds for a long time and I had them with me. One night, looking up at the moon, I decided that starting the next day, I would sow my seeds. Some Mexicans told me that the best place to sow pot seeds was in dried-up river beds. So I started out and for about three months, I walked an average of eight miles a day. And at the end I had an estimated million plants growing. I was Johnny Appleseed. I would find fertile beds and throw them out there. If they grew, they grew. If they didn't, I would forget about it. Takes too much time when it comes to cultivating them. Besides the police, you have little bugs.

Since I had been in the Sierras for about four months, I only saw the plants get to maybe a foot. I'm sure there's still a lot growing up there now. Those plants just took off. It's so fertile up there that the plants started popping up everywhere. But no telling how much would have died in two months from lack of water, you know, things like this. But I figure there probably would have been maybe a thousand pounds that I could've gotten out. Would've been about a hundred dollars a pound.

That was the end of '69 when I was doing that. Somehow the narcs found out about what I was doing and that's when the shit hit the fan. I got turned into a narcotics agent. They couldn't even begin to believe where I had been. They were screwed up so bad when they pulled the warrant on me that I got off the whole thing. Since I was camped way up in the Sierras, I'd taken lots of supplies, and different people were scheduled to go up and see me at certain times. But the weekend they went to bust me, my friends came up and we moved my camp. A woman had come to stay with me for a couple of weeks, you know, 'cause it was really getting nice up there. The narcs came in on a Monday morning and busted me in my new camp. But the warrant had the wrong date on it, and that's what got me off.

They were really, really down on me. They had helicopters. You know, they tried to make deals with me like, "We'll let you off, we'll do anything, just tell us where you were." And I said, "No man, you're going to have to prove it. I already know I'm getting off." And the chick, they busted her too for possession, but she got off because they had a bad warrant for me. And then they made me leave. They kicked me right out.

As a matter of fact, I left the Sierras and for the next four months I went to court. I had a really good lawyer. A local lawyer. He cost me $1,500. I had friends who came up from the San Francisco area. They put up $3,750 cash bail. County had never even seen that kind of money. I got it all back for them the next week. It was all very easy and simple as long as I simply worked in the system. And they worked in it, too.

Well, after that, my mother decided that I needed pretty much of a rest. My sister lives in Hawaii, so they sent me over there. They paid my plane fare and sent me over there with the intentions of working with my brother-in-law on his boat. He's got a fishing boat there. They live on the island of Maui, and I didn't really dig that too much, living with her, because she's a Jesus freak and that's too much for me to handle. So I ran across this job at a dairy, milking cows. They gave me three dollars an hour, a house with thirteen acres of land and three bedrooms. I worked seven days in a row, got a day and a half off, worked eight days, got five days off and it was great. Great place, great experience there. For a year and a half I did that, before I came over here.

It was kind of lonely on the farm but I had a few women. I skip from girl to girl, you know. If she feels good for a year, it's for a year. If she feels good for a night, it's a night. I found one that felt good for a long time, felt great. I don't push nothing on women, just let them do what they want to do. Basically because that's what I want to do. Any kind of a grasp is the way people start to pull away from relationships.

I lived with a woman who had a five-year-old girl. She was . . . really something. This woman was raised in Japan; she was a top student, went to University of Colorado, got it on with a black dude and had a baby. Which doesn't mean much, but it says a lot, you know, as far as freedom and hang-ups. Then somebody took her kid and split to Hawaii. Stole the baby and split to Hawaii. She went after him and she ended up staying in Hawaii. Since I had extra room at the house, I told her that if she needed a place to stay, she could move in. This was after we had gone to bed together. It's something that just flowed together, came together.

I'm a very emotional person as far as awareness. If I feel like crying, I cry, you know. I don't hold nothing back as far as emotions go. You know you've got to let them get out or they hurt you, maybe even destroy you. I had this experience of taking LSD and seeing through my third eye. I don't know if you've talked to any people who've experienced this, but it's not only happening in India, it's happening in California, too. People who are into a scientific trip find out who they really are through cleaning themselves and deculturizing so that their life chemicals can flow. Then you can bliss. You universally center yourself. You use what faculties you've been given instead of being computerized, culturized to use only a certain part of it. These people are learning that they don't have to protect themselves from anything. There's nothing here to protect themselves from. They call themselves The Center People and they are in a relationship with the Maharaj Ji. These people say that everybody has their own turn-on charge of electricity that makes you flow. If you can charge that electricity, you can become equal with equal. You know, what is it that we do every day that's not cultural? Nothing. Maybe sleeping, but sleeping could be cultural.

LSD helped me to understand these ideas. But I've taken LSD too many times. Maybe three hundred. I know it too well, what it does. I know what the limitations of it are; that's why I don't take it any more. Because of the plastic hangover behind it. It's just that LSD is so real. The clarity, the feeling of being there before, the feeling of truth, straight, you know, it is like that. Just clarity—something I'd never felt—really peace for maybe three or four days afterward too.

LSD can bring you a lot of good feelings. One time it brought me levitation. And bliss. And changing through talking to people. And feeling emotions. And feeling aware. LSD can put you in such a blissful state of being that you feel like you're air.

LSD helps you to come together. You begin to understand that the only thing you need is what the culture forces you to need. I'm not going to play that game. I'm going back to a place where there's no passport hassles, no visa hassles, no Indians coming out from behind trees, no Afghanis asking what your name is. I'm going back to the mountains for a while. I'm going back to the States. Back to California. I've just been away a year.

I can clean out there. Means to get rid of loneliness, feeling lonely. Instead of feeling lonely you feel good about feeling lonely. You feel good about just being with the trees. I'll spend my day in the mountains walking, just walking. And as I walk, I'll think that everybody's trip is their own illusion.

I want to be able to bliss when I want to bliss. I want to be able to bliss with other people because I am blissing, because we are the same. I'd like to see other people come back to it, if that's what it is. If that's not my own illusion. I just have to go somewhere other than where people are, really. We're all alone in this world, so we find what we need to adapt and to survive alone. Otherwise it's all frustration. To me, that's how I feel. The first time I was alone in the wilderness, I learned what loneliness was. I learned that I could be really happy out there, almost in a blissful state, where I didn't even know what was happening really. And I just felt really good, uh, talking to a tree, talking to myself. No drugs, just me.

I'm trying to get out of a physical trip. I won't even ball chicks anymore, on the level that they want to be balled on. Because of the cultural part of it, for me my existence is this. I'm a human being. I'm walking down the street. There's a woman there. Something starts feeling good in my lower area. And I'm driving toward her. She feels the rhythm, the vibrations, coming. She turns. Maybe she rejects it. Maybe she flows with it. If she flows with it, it's done right there. It's gone through with. But I can't do it that way because you have to go here to fuck. And fuck this way. On your back. You know how it is. It's all culture. We've never had a chance to really fuck freely. Now I hear if you go up here in the backwoods in Afghanistan you might be able to fuck a Koochi girl. The koochis are the wild women of the wanderers in Afghanistan. They're like dogs, you know. They run. They fuck each other. They play very freely with each other. When they're kids, they're kissing.

Why do we have to differentiate ourselves from animals? Thinking, to me, is what slows us down from using our senses. I don't care about thinking. That doesn't even exist where I'm coming from. Do you know how much energy we cut off from our feet just by wearing shoes? A lot of people I get into this conversation with and I feel that there's not too many you can lay these trips on because they can't grasp onto it very fast. Some people it takes a couple of months of being around an individual that's been into it. But we're living in a really superficial place. When a man becomes president and at the end of his time he's dead, what can you say, except that his ego was satisfied. Even so he's still dead.

People have to realize that a person's life is only precious to the beholder. If people die, they die. I think we've been saving too many people, that's what I think. I think life is the same as death. It's all a rush. People here just live, die. Live, die. There's nothing really wrong with that except from where we come from. Where everybody has to live a good life. But who's to say what the good life is. I think they're all screwed up, and nobody knows what the good life really is. I don't think I do either, but I think I've made an approach toward it just by being able to feel bliss and bliss with other people, the feeling of love.

The feeling of being loose, free, feeling loneliness, feeling clear, the woodsy feeling, perky feeling. Then going to Hawaii, the same feeling. I was alone for five months in that house. You know, you look at yourself a lot, and then you have to break out your thing. But when it breaks for you, you're down to such a place with nature that you break into the ozone, so to speak. You find out afterward that any trip is simply a trip; there's nothing good or bad about it.

Like Christ. Jesus Christ was just a regular human being that was operating in ozone. He was right there. He could do anything because he was in tune.

We're so cultured that it's an effort to get to bed with a woman, and that frustration alone taps on your brain, takes energy. I just don't fuck anymore. And I don't miss it. As a matter of fact, I'm just raising energy consciousness and thinking. I don't really use drugs. I just smoke hash. The thing you smoke chillum for is the physical rush that the tobacco gives you in the beginning. It keeps you stoned for a long time. I've been tripping on eight grams of hash oil. You know what hash oil is? Eighty to ninety percent. Hash is only seventy percent. The best way is to mix it with tea and honey. And it's very different. It's like being drunk. The thinking in that realm is pretty much like the realm of blissing, very clear. People here, they smoke hash and they only get a little high. This flows through your whole body. You can walk down the street and almost float. It's like being drunk, you lose your equilibrium a little bit.

I think living should be like floating. Like the family. All of us need to come closer together, and be more honest with our kids, not playing so many games with them, turning them onto good things to do, you know, in their childhood. Like raising dogs. Or playing with cats. Playing with animals. You know, just let it all hang out with your kids. Just give yourself to them.

I think highly of the way my mother raised me, as to how she related to my independent feelings. You know, even when I did things that were totally unreal to her, for instance, just coming in blasted drunk, falling over the kitchen table, she was good. She was sort of passive, said, "He's just a kid, you know." She didn't tell me to go away or get lost. She just made the best of it. I lived with a grandmother, too. And a great grandmother, as a matter of fact. And an aunt, to start off with. From the time I was eight to fourteen. My great grandmother was eighty-six. She came across to California in one of the covered wagons. In the 1800's she was just a little girl. We're an extension of a famous family a little bit. But those are all historical facts, you know. They make my identity and makes it easier for you now to relate to me. Now, all that stuff I've told you about my mother is lies. Now how do you relate to me? As a human being?

Fortunately, three of the women I lived with had babies, young babies, very small, up to five. The five-year-old was much better because there was more communication. She's only five, but she likes sex. She likes smoking hash better than pot. At five. She also participates in sexual activities like fucking and blowing me.

Yeah, kids can. It's only in our heads that we think it's weird, bad, freak-out, you know. It freaked me out because I wasn't really aware that it happened. I really hadn't been thinking about a small human being being able to do something like that. But it's done here all the time. In Tibet, it's done all the time. And in the States it's starting to happen. There's a lot of things going on in the States with little kids. Some people look at them as immoral acts, you know. But over here most people feel it's a natural act. Like playing dolls wasn't any different from sucking dick. Make it feel the best you can, and give it the most. And, you know, be good. That's all we were trying to teach her.

Now, I lived with these people, I lived with the girl for seven months. And I saw the little girl go through the change of fantasy. It was a neat thing. A new toy, you know: "Can I turn you on," "Can I make you feel good?" Then she started saying, "Will you buy me candy if I give you head?" She was told that was nowhere, man. What kind of bullshit is that? At the age of seven she can hit the road. She can go wherever she wants to go. She doesn't have any hang-ups of her mother saying stay till you're eighteen. It's like get the fuck out of here, kid. Go do your trip, man. You know, what's going to happen to her? Nothing but freedom. She's being educated. She's smarter than most of the kids in her school already. You know, what can you do about it? Now she's smarter toward history, geography. But maybe she'll be more into geography because she travels around on her own. And she has to know where she's going. She's going to be dynamite. Her mother's like Kim Novak.

They're not my kids. I have no responsibility. If a girl wants the kid, she takes the kid, if she doesn't, then she puts it somewhere where it can grow up, but in our culture, everybody's supposed to relate to mother, father. It's all a matter of his freedom to me, in the end, and how he can adjust to the structure and still have his freedom.

That kid won't have my hang-ups. My cultural hang-ups. I just want to cut off the culture. I want to cut off all existence we've known. I want to cut off having to think about living, saving lives, pollution, cut out all that stuff because it really doesn't exist. It only exists where the culture has made it exist, or where it has existed in the culture for years.

We have to adapt. I'm trying to adapt, in another completely impossible way than other people could think about. But that's my hang-up. Dig it? And I have to live with the fact that I have responsibility. But I say I don't because I just don't look at it as responsibility, it's just that this is what I have to do. What more can I say?

Robert is adaptable. You met him working in a factory. You met him farming in Hawaii. We met him tripping out on metaphysics in the East. Could we all meet him motorcycling as a Hell's Angel? Could we meet him making dirty movies?

His profoundly amoral attitude reflects his lack of humanistic or ethical values. Robert's life is his illusion.

18 Mr. Klein

"Oh, screw it, I want to own my own feelings."

Tired, ashen-faced forty-one-year-old Mr. Klein sat behind his desk. He was there with the carpet on the floor, the secretary outside the door, the big desk and the shelves with books. And the benefits. In other words, an executive. A decision maker.

He lived in a very expensive suburb. He was married and had a daughter and a son.

Well, we moved to the suburbs five years ago for a variety of reasons. In the city, we lived in an integrated co-op. It was, you know, a good apartment, reasonable. It seemed to be a planned community. We moved there and thought it would be very nice. We were very pleased that it was a cooperative experience, both economically and socially, and the schools would be new. There was talk of an educational park. We moved in there with a kind of hope that it would mean a better life for all of us.

I became disenchanted bit by bit over the years, disenchanted because of the tremendous conflict between the Jewish middle class and the black people. The whole thing was really triggered when Martin Luther King was assassinated. There was a lot of anger spilling out and a lot of white kids were beaten up. My kids never directly suffered from it, but there was a lot of tension in the community and there was a beginning split between black and white. Then the teachers' strike came along and most of the white people supported the teachers. A few didn't. I didn't. I slept in the school. I thereby became closer to some of the black militants in the community and I felt good about that except that there was a great deal of dissension in the community. We were active in insurgent Democratic politics. We were active in civil rights.

But the violence continued. There were a number of rapes in the project and a murder. My daughter was getting older; I was worried about her traveling in the community though she handled herself pretty well.

About three years before I had been mugged in New York, and I had been seriously hurt. Then my friend was robbed twice in the parking lot and I was afraid to come home late at night. So we reluctantly moved out of the community. Of course we rationalized it with, you know, well, the community wasn't so great anyway. But we fled from danger.

We went into a safer situation where there wasn't the threat of bodily harm and where we had easier access to the community—and my daughter, Debbie, could walk around. My son, Alan, was immediately relieved when we moved into the suburbs; it was evident. Alan was eight then, and Debbie was eleven. And, I felt kind of guilty about it. A lot of my friends who still lived in the city said, "Oh, cop-outs. There go the ex-white liberals."

And I really didn't give a damn after a while because I said, "Look, in this world a person has to save himself." If I can't live in that community, if I'm full of fear, my family is full of fear, we can't function, then I can't deal with principles any more. And anyway I guess I have to admit the mugging really shook me up. It put into me a kind of fear that I had never had before and I could never escape it.

So we moved out to this suburb which is, you know, a dumping ground for radicals and liberals who want to escape these problems. And I've been very happy living in this suburb. I like the ambience—the freedom, the movement, the interesting people. Over the years I've been politically active. All my progressive friends from the city moved out to my suburb. The school system there is as good as any school system can be. It gives the opportunities for some innovations. There are a lot of teachers who are very creative. We have alternative campuses and my daughter participates in one of them. And there's a lot of concern for growing human awareness—the Women's Liberation movement is flourishing.

But, of course, it also suffers from all the problems of a golden Jewish ghetto because it is probably about seventy percent Jewish; there are more minorities moving in. I noticed the figures the other day. In the school system, ten percent of our kids are black, about three percent are Puerto Rican, about one percent Indian. So we have some mixture; it's not pure white. But the primary tone of the community is that of relatively affluent white middle class. That has some consequences. It's a community where wealth is evident and places pressure on you. It's a community where the kind of political activity is on this fund-raising, lawn-party, or fancy house-party level. But I have some very close friends in the community, very close, and many acquaintances with whom I find a lot in common who live rather modestly in spite of all this, and who are pursuing what's important to them.

Well, this has had a positive effect on my kids. If they had always lived there I wouldn't say that, but they've had the experience of living elsewhere, in poorer surroundings, in mixed surroundings. They didn't have as many rich friends as they have now. But my daughter is very independent and she uses the resources of the community very well. She doesn't have a fixed school program; she takes what she wants, and she can get individual attention from her teachers. She's interested in dance, and that's what she pursues. Also there are a lot of kids who come from homes where the people are pretty well educated. There's a high degree of understanding about the changing values in society; I suspect perhaps there's less alienation between parents and kids in many families there than in other communities. Because the parents themselves are really part of this revolution. A lot of them, you know, have played around with smoking pot. Of course, these are just surface vestiges. But a lot of them are interested in alternative forms of education and participate in it. I participate in the School Executive Committee and my wife, Leslie, does too. We meet a lot of people that way. People come to adult-ed classes—we have a terrific adult-ed program. I run a consciousness-raising group. That got a tremendous reception and it's being repeated.

Well, our consciousness-raising group is usually a leaderless situation in which eight to fourteen people—men only or women only—get together to discuss issues in society that relate to their functioning as a man or a woman and discuss it in terms of their feelings. It's an attempt to achieve a greater amount of self-awareness, away from roles. As you deal with those feelings on a very personal level you attempt to expand your consciousness and awareness and thereby increase your enjoyment of life, the quality of your personal relationships.

So we had a series of sessions. You get together. Either you set up topics to discuss or people deal with their feelings about things that bother them or certain rules that they follow—not to interrupt, not to be overly judgmental, not to be destructive, not to be therapeutic in any sense other than asking questions to gain greater understanding about what a person is talking about . . . there's a lot of that going on in our suburb.

People are into themselves because all their institutions are falling down and a great many people I know are aware of this, and are confused by it. They see their kids being turned off by the schools. They see their kids turning to drugs, and drugs are rampant in our suburb and have been all along.

Debbie's friends are primarily white. This is an insulation

that Debbie rebels against. Of course she has been sucked into this wealthy kind of life style. A large number of her friends are very wealthy, very spoiled kids. And she wants things. This places pressure on us. She used to like dungarees, but now she wants much more expensive clothing.

My son, Alan, feels more secure in our suburb. He's happier because he can get on his bike and ride everywhere. He's not worried about being accosted by tough kids. In school he feels more relaxed.

But I think all the kids must feel insulated. I've never spoken to them directly about it. First of all, they're repelled by the Jewish renaissance, the opulence, the concern with material things. There are contradictions. They reject the notion of couples. They never move as a boy and a girl; they always move in groups. They neglect the notion of middle-class morality; they often go skinny-dipping in the pools. They travel a lot. They go camping on their own; they take long trips for rock concerts; they all go to out-of-town colleges; they travel for the summer. Debbie wants to travel again this summer; she wants to hitchhike to friends in Denver. I tell her she's only seventeen, and we're opposed to her hitchhiking. With Debbie, because we've cut down the amount of conflict by not dealing with every issue that comes up, we find she fights us less on an issue like that. We let Debbie completely manage her own financial affairs, her hours, when she goes out. When she stays out very late she has to call us at two and let us know what's what. We provide some structure, but she has a lot of freedom. My wife and I went to therapy and dealt with our own problems and fears about Debbie. We're pretty honest with her. We do a lot of talking about things and Debbie doesn't feel that we're laying a trip on her but that we're telling her how we feel, and we listen to her. But in certain matters she has no choice. That's just it if she continues to live in our house. We usually come up with an effective compromise.

Debbie is always frank with us about sex. I guess we encouraged it. And, I was very surprised at my own reaction. I know the first time Debbie ever got into a heavy petting session, she was less than thirteen. I didn't get terribly upset, although I always thought I'd be a possessive father.

We were away in the country, at a place. She was fooling around with someone we knew, and I just found her in the room. I surmised what happened. I never asked Debbie directly. And she never told me directly. But I surmised that they actually had intercourse.

My wife, Leslie, says that premarital sex is okay, but with her own daughter she's got a problem. I think premarital sex is okay, even with Debbie, but, you know, within certain contexts. So, we had discussions with her like just don't go and screw with anybody; it's gotta be significant; it's gotta be part of something; sex is an important expression in a good relationship; and you have to be careful when you have sex; don't exploit yourself; don't get knocked up. And Debbie became very frank. She used to tell me, "Boy, I'd like to go to bed with that guy." I tried to slip in my points, unobtrusively, but I never said flat out, "You can't have sexual relations." Leslie got disturbed once because Debbie had a boy in the house and the door was closed and the lights were out and it seemed as though something was happening. Leslie said, "You just can't do those kind of things in the house. Not because you can't do them outside, but it bothers me. You have to respect that, you know, it's like I'm condoning your doing that." And Leslie's position was always that. She doesn't condone it. She thinks it's wrong. She thinks Debbie's too young. But she's obviously in conflict about it, because she took Debbie out when she was sixteen and got her a diaphragm at the clinic, which is a very good thing for her to have done. I suspect most of Debbie's friends are not virgins, and they're all between sixteen and seventeen.

Alan has a lot of free sexual discussions and I'm very helpful about it. There was a little problem with Alan asking, so I asked him where he was at with girls. I never do it in any intense way, any embarrassing way.

He may be into masturbation but I don't think he's into girls. I'm not sure but I haven't seen any evidence of it. Though he does like the bathroom . . . He's a great kid, my Alan, really great.

I'm very mixed up. I don't even know what the hell I want for myself. I think my kids know that I'm mixed up, that I'm trapped, and that I am the product of how I was brought up. They know that I'm really not terribly interested in my present life. If I could only get past my hang-up of looking for people's approval and having to, you know, get some status from the work ethic. What's important to me is the whole notion of really experiencing life, existentially, really being turned on by ideas and having the leisure just to sit and look at things and to think about them.

My kids hear me talk to Leslie about them and they know that I'm always into something like consciousness-raising or therapy and they know that Leslie and I are very intensely involved in a therapy group now which is having a significant impact on us. And they know that I don't want them to live the way I have lived; that I want them to get in touch with how they feel about things, and how they view life, and to live in a way that's meaningful to them.

But I'm not really living for myself.

I can cut myself off from all my neurotic interactions with the world I live in. I really don't give a shit about status, and having a position, making a lot of money and being the good stud with the women and being respected and being thought of as intelligent. I really don't give a shit about that because it doesn't do a goddamn thing for me. It's not that I don't want to use my mind; it's not that I don't want to screw; it's not that I don't want to be a man in the relationship with a woman, but I want to redefine all those things. I am, in therapy, trying to cut off all those things. I'm trying to cut off the notion that *I* control all the finances in my family because a man does that; *I* have to support the family because a man does that; *I* have to make sure the woman has a good orgasm because a man is really servicing the woman sexually—he has to prove something to himself and unless he can have her have that good orgasm and have an orgasm himself, he's not a man.

What I want is to get in touch with my own feelings and to do what I want to do. And that may mean not working. Or not making all the money. Leslie could make some of the money. Making adjustments, not living in a big house, living in a shack if that makes me happy. Whatever it is that I want to do I want to be free to do it and I don't want to care what people think about me. I want a woman who lives with me because she wants to live with me and I want children who are free to explore the world for themselves in terms of how they can appreciate and feel about it in an honest way.

I'm scared shitless to do it. Look at my kids. They sit there—seventeen and fourteen—and I have to send them to college. I don't *have* to. But I've been conditioned to believe that I have to send them to college, so I have to earn money for that.

No, I don't *have* to, intellectually. Emotionally, I can't change that goddamn feeling. But I have changed some things. Like, I've given Leslie charge of all the finances which takes away a sense of power from me and I feel lonely because of it. But I've given it to her and it's entirely up to her. I don't want to say anything about it unless I find a Cadillac in my driveway and no food on the table. I dropped a lot of competitive feelings I had in my work. I do my work and if it turns out well that's fine. And if I'm fired that's the way it is. I don't want to be hung up because of my job. Oh, screw it, I want to own my own feelings.

I'm exploring my inner space. And I want to map it. I want to understand it and I want to expand my sensory appreciation of the world. I want to explore myself. And that's not an egocentric trip. But I mean it only in the sense that I want to get to know how I really feel about things and get rid of all that programming that's been imposed on me. I've had twenty-five years of marriage and I don't think that I've gotten out of it what I could have gotten out of it. I think I've made those years pretty rotten for myself and for my wife but I'll only take responsibility for myself. That's all I can . . . and for my kids. And I'm very confused; I feel very ignorant, and I want to learn more.

When I talk to Alan and he gets angry I've learned to stop responding to his anger by saying, ''What the hell are you angry about?'' Or, ''You may be angry but you gotta do this.'' That's a violation of his feelings. I say to him, ''Alan, I see you're upset. Could you tell me what you're upset about.'' You know, accept the kid's feelings and get him to try to deal with them.

Well, I'm very trapped by things. I have a house, a lot of bills and I keep taking on more all the time. At my job, I keep getting sucked into more and more programs. Rather than freeing myself, I'm constrained more and more. I've done one thing which breaks away from this. I bought this country house with three other couples and we go to therapy together. And I can see that that's a beginning break. Like a number of years from now I could leave this and go and live there and do something there in order to earn a little bread to survive. It's not *going* someplace else that makes it better. But if I can reconstruct myself in this new environment that would make it better. It's very hard for me to make the break. I'm still going through therapy and I'm still afraid. I may come out of this not wanting to continue my relationship with Leslie. She has the same viewpoint. I'm not in this to improve my relationship. I'm in this to deal with myself, save myself. I feel very desperate at this point in my life. I guess it's the middle-age malaise of looking back and saying, ''What the hell have I done?'' And feeling very, very desperate because there is not much ahead yet. There are so many defeated dreams. Illusions are falling by the wayside and you have to face the fact that you're gonna die in not too many years. And it's all been a meaningless thing.

I suppose that's part of it and I think that also because I'm growing up a little bit. I'm getting away. I think I've been looking for mama love all these years. I'm getting away from it. And my mind is wide open to a million things, a million possibilities in living patterns, in vocational pursuits. That's the kind of free, wide-open environment, I think, in which my kids live. My kids live that way. Debbie hardly ever eats with us. And Alan, of course, still has more time with us although he's beginning to express his independence. And Leslie, of course, is completely self-involved, in her pottery especially. So that we have a fluid house, which has always been a problem to me. It's threatening to me. People aren't playing their roles. Leslie isn't being the mother and the kids aren't being kids; they're being individuals. And I don't know how to be an individual. So because of *them* they cause me great pain and unhappiness.

But it's *my* problem, really. I mean, Debbie causes me pain by the fact that she isn't here. She wants to be free. Sometimes when I come home she doesn't talk to me, because she's involved with something. She causes me pain by not talking to me, by not paying attention to me, by not recognizing my father role as I understand it to be. Leslie does the same thing because she doesn't reinforce the husband role that I see as being the important role to play with a woman. I think I said to her in therapy about two months ago, I said, "I've been such a good boy all through my married life and yet you keep rejecting me."

Well, she didn't say anything. I was expressing my feelings and I wanted to say, "That's the goddamn problem." Why do I have to be a good boy in a married relationship?

I've been terribly hurt in my relationships because I always felt I was giving and giving and giving. But I've really been very selfish. I wanted Debbie to give me feedback as a daughter and Leslie to give me feedback as a wife. I was looking for their approval. And that's what I'm trying to turn around.

Debbie doesn't dump her problems on me. She handles herself in a very mature way for a seventeen-year-old girl. She's really a sweet kid. Like the other night I mentioned that I was low on pot, so she said, "I've got some pot that's very expensive." I said, "Gee, Deb, I can't right now. Your mother just paid the bills and I'm broke." So she said, "Don't worry, dad, look, let me get some pot and I'll work it out so that you can pay when you want to. Let me help you out." It's not terribly important. It's the whole notion that she would help me because she felt that I couldn't take care of it. I found it touching, that she was concerned about me. Or, one night I was talking about Alan and I said, "Boy, Debbie, did I handle Alan terribly tonight. I really botched the whole goddamn thing." And she said, "Yeah, dad, I'd really like to talk about it; I'd like to make some suggestions but I have an appointment. I have to go out. I would like to talk to you about it later. Is that okay?"

You know, I don't know how to handle my anger like if Alan calls me "Fuck." You know, it's not the name, but I feel put down by it which is absurd.

I was always very permissive about drugs. We were very frank with Debbie. We told Debbie when she was about fourteen that Leslie infrequently smoked pot. And I smoke pot fairly regularly. Not every day, but weekends, one night a week. You know, instead of drinking scotch, I smoke pot. When Debbie started to smoke pot, Leslie was frantic. Debbie and I talked about our experiences with pot. I tried to make the point that as long as you don't have a dependency on it, it's okay.

I have a friend, Dave. He's younger than me. My daughter apparently told him she had taken acid when she was out on the coast last summer and he encouraged her to tell me. Leslie doesn't know, but Debbie told me and I reacted to it very well. I asked her about it and what it was like. Then we discussed the dangers and so on. So she said, "I don't think I'm going to take it any more. It's frightening. But I had to." So I said, "Okay, that's good." And she had taken it a couple of times. And I said I had taken it, too. I was very honest about it. I said I was confused about drugs. I think they're dangerous, although I can see the attraction to them and they may have some medical purposes. A hallucinogenic drug under therapeutic guidance may be a very beneficial thing. I don't know. I never got terribly excited about it. I gave her a great deal of license.

If she smokes cigarettes, if she takes drugs, if she has sexual relationships . . . these are expressions of her own needs and desires, which are not going to destroy her in the sense that she's going to die. But I tell her if you quit school and you don't have skills, that limits the kind of life you can have.

I was lower middle class. I was brought up to think that education was important. I was the only one in my family that had a college education. Everyone was very happy and they constantly reinforced the notion that I had to be a good boy. By being very neat, by listening to my mother. I grew up in an extended family because my mother and my father separated when I was a year old. Then my mother remarried a number of years later. So I lived with my grandmother and aunt and uncle and my mother and a friend. My stepfather wasn't on the scene then. So, I was a very good boy and I was wanting to be a good boy because I got good feedback. So I was well behaved, was very neat, listened to my mother, said prayers at night. I had a lot of affection for people. I shared everything I had. I could break a piece of gum into ten pieces and give them to ten people. I always wanted approval. I went to school because that was the right thing to do. I always helped in the house because that was correct. I always made a living. I was always there with my kids because that was the correct thing to do and I was always a very sweet, nice person. I mean, I would take people home. Everybody could depend on me.

I was a schmuck . . . because I never did anything for myself. I did things to get people's approval.

Putting all the intellectual bullshit aside, I realize now that I am a very weak, vacillating man. But ultimately what I am still trying to define is exactly what I want. But I'll tell you one thing: if I had it to do all over again, I would never live my life the way I have. First of all, I would have married later. And I doubt that I would have married the same woman. But . . . well . . . that's another story.

Mr. Klein has apparently surrendered his authority to his children. To varying degrees, many parents today do just that. Any youngster needs boundaries which limit what he can and cannot do. Without such limits the child's self-identity is threatened and his character weakened.

In an affluent society, it is easy to give. It is always harder to withhold. Thus many of the young people with whom we spoke had had too much too soon. It was as if they had compressed fifty years of living into twenty. What was left to experience?

Unfortunately, Mr. Klein had very little sense of his own

strengths and of the importance of passing these strengths on to his children. The sharing of the ten pieces of gum with ten different people is one aspect of this strength. The commitment to getting an education is another. In short, historically there are values within the American middle-class tradition which should be passed on to our children: orderliness, hard work, thrift, a commitment to learning and acquiring skills. To disown one's basic values, as Mr. Klein has done, is to rob one's children of part of their fundamental birthright.

As we talked and interviewed middle-class youngsters in the United States and in Afghanistan, we became convinced that many youngsters had had no strong authority figure in their lives. Many of them had practically grown up without parents. Therefore, there were few internalized constraints. Their attitude was very often: "Anything goes."

Thus when Mr. Klein says that he wants "to own his own feelings," we must realize that we learn that from people around us. If the parents repress their feelings about what they think is right and appropriate behavior then the youngster will also be confused. Truly, he won't know *what* to think. And if that confusion is compounded by a lack of discipline, we create a kind of psychological nomad who will wander aimlessly through Zen, gurus, LSD, Christianity, mysticism, yoga, and on.

Ultimately, all we have to give to our children is ourselves. That is our most precious contribution to them. And since we are fallible, we will also transmit some of our prejudices and personal failings. But the fear of "making a mistake" should not force us to the self-abnegating position of Mr. Klein. We are better than that. So is he.

19 Chuck

"I mean I leave my head alone, so should everybody else."

We found Chuck sitting alone at a regulars' table at The Wishing Well. He gave us a big smile as we walked over to him. He was wearing jeans, construction boots, a plaid flannel shirt, and a braided leather headband.

"My hair? I do it like this once a week. I wash it and part it in the middle and put this headband on. I can't keep it from frizzing out—but at least this keeps it out of my eyes."

I spent most of my developing years in this "burb." My family moved here when I was about five or so. When I got to high school they sent me to a private military school. Don't know if it was so they could straighten me out or because this rich burb has good schools and everyone has a lot of money. Most kids go here to school so you must be like super rich if you

197

send your kids away to school. I think my old lady was happy, though. I was one less for her to deal with. She has enough to do keeping up with my old man and his demands. You know, she doesn't even drive a car. He likes keeping her under his thumb. There's not much to say about my high school experience. I do remember one time when this upperclassman was really hassling me and I had had it so I beat the shit out of him. Of course the dude reported me and then I was thoroughly abused by the head. They suspended me from school for that.

College was great. I got a classic T-Bird for a graduation present from high school, so I commuted to college. My parents paid for everything and I hardly ever went. Caro, my girl, went to school out here and I kept all my grade school friends so I used to get up early and pile in the bird and come uptown and hang out with my friends. Most of them were into cutting, too. Like hunting and fishing are what I did most of college. A couple of the guys and I had a little boat and we used to go duck hunting. They have great ducks around here. We used to take a lot of shit and beer with us and sit out in the boat all day and once in a while this great duck would go by and bang. It was great. Half the fun was avoiding the hassles. I mean here we'd be in the bay going bang, bang. And some lady would hear these shots in her kitchen and call the cops. They were always lecturing us on how dangerous it was to be hunting in a populated area. It was such a goof because nobody here ever goes near the bay. They were just afraid of guns. We found out it wasn't against the law to duck hunt. We made sure to have a license, so they started yelling at us for trespassing on property to get to the bay.

One of the guys who owned the boat with me, my partner, his property was a little on the bay, so we'd walk through there. We had to be careful, though, because he was cutting, too. We'd have to make sure his mother wasn't home. We even used to eat the ducks. His mother worked so we'd go in the kitchen and clean the duck and eat him. Anyway, we hung around a lot and did a lot of dope and good things like that. It was great times. I "attended" college for three years. But then I was supposed to be graduating the next year, and my dad asked how I was doing and what was I gonna do when I got out? He finally checked with the school and found out that I only had eighteen credits for three years of his money. He couldn't believe that.

He and my uncles are rich. They own this huge business. I always figured money was never gonna be a problem. So my old man gave me this heavy rap about paying my own way, and my mother was all upset about my being a bum, so I work for this company on and off. I do like construction work and get paid very well for doing very little. I still live at home. My mother cooks for me, but I'm only there for short periods of time. I sleep at home and eat most meals at home and shower there and my old lady does my dirty laundry. I don't talk to my father anymore, not for years. What little we do say shouldn't be repeated. We walk past one another and say nothing. We eat meals together and once in a while it may be, "Pass the sugar"—but no please.

My mother spends most of her life in the kitchen. Sometimes I drive her so she can do the shopping. Sometimes she tries to talk to me. She hates it when I come up here, the "Drinking Hole." Sometimes when I go home loaded she wakes up and yells. She tries. I can give her credit. God bless mothers. I think she can guess vaguely what I'm into. Once she took this trip to California. I have this joke with her. I ask her if she "found herself out on the Coast?" No matter how many times I say that, she always laughs.

I like it when people laugh. Things are much better when they are kept mellow, you know, soft. You know, I have a good reputation. Ask anyone. They all know Chuck. I make them laugh and never get into anything heavy. I have a way of making people my friends. But never heavy. They like it that way. I also can do a lot of stuff and function. Like I can drink a quart of gin, do two or three downs, take mescaline, and still function. And it's not a drag on anybody.

Oh, once in a great while a friend of mine takes me home to

my spare time. At the present time I'm having this contest with one of my friends to catch the "elusive bluefish." I'm a real "Captain Blueballs." Sometimes at night if it's slow here and Caro's not seeing me, I go fishing by myself. Get a little stoned and take some beers and the boat and go out alone. I almost got the mermaid a couple times. If I float into this one spot I see her. It's no joke. She sits on the shore and waves to me. Wow, is she fantastic. Looks like one of those TV commercials. You know, all hazy and foggy with the blond hair shining and a secret smile, just for me. One time she got off the rock and started swimming to me and I started rowing toward her and it was like a movie. The two of us floating toward one another, and when I could almost touch her, she swam away. Son-of-a-bitch. Never saw anybody swim so fast in all my life. You know how all fishermen tell about the one that got away? Well, the mermaid got away, but someday I'm gonna get her, no lie.

Why should I get into heavy raps and worry about "the future"? Life's been pretty good so far. This other friend of mine, the boat partner. Well, he's got a big family and two of them are sisters. The older one is divorced with two kids and she lives in the city. And I see her once in a while. One time she came in here to see her brother and I was leaning on the bar, just watching. And she said, "What do you see?" and I said, "People drinking." "Are they having a good time?" she asks. "I don't know. They just come here." "Why?" she asks. Well, I must've been a little down 'cause we got into this heavy rap about it, and she really made me think. Then the younger sister and I have been good friends for years and one other time she starts this same shit, and like I keep telling them I can't take it. I mean those two broads are really smart and I have a lot of respect for them, but they shouldn't fuck my head like that. I don't want to get into any of that shit. I mean like I told one of them I'd give her 826 hub caps if she'd give me back my mind. I mean I leave my head alone, so should everybody else.

True to his self-image, Chuck never let our conversation with him get too heavy. As we saw it, the problem with Chuck was that he had never had to fight for anything. There was no struggle in his life. Everything had been given to him and would be given to him in the future. He had no desires. No beliefs. He was without passion, as so many of his suburban contemporaries seem to be. There was no steel in his character and there probably never would be unless there was some cataclysmic event in his life. Chuck was like putty—soft, malleable, easy-going, standing for nothing. Indeed, Chuck would leave his head alone as well as everyone else's.

20   Mrs. McLoughlin

"Tolerance—in the broad sense of the word—as in to understand."

Mrs. McLoughlin is in her late forties. She is the mother of a
large family. Her children range in age from eighteen to thirty.
Her youngest son is a senior in high school. Several are of
college age. Two are married and one is divorced. She has four
grandchildren.

She is the daughter of emigrant parents who raised her in their
ethnic traditions.

She graduated from high school at the age of fifteen and
wanted to enter college. There she thought she would study
medicine and become a doctor. However, her parents found this
unacceptable and insisted that she attend a finishing school.
She obeyed.

While attending finishing school, she fell in love with one of her
professors. They married. She continued her education but did
not graduate. Her first child was born.

During World War II, her husband volunteered and served in the Pacific theater. When he returned from service, he was a confirmed alcoholic. Shortly thereafter, this led to their divorce.

She met her second husband a few years later at a party. Over the next years, they had four more children. During their years of marriage, Mr. McLoughlin's job entailed a lot of travel. The family was forced to move every year. After fourteen years of marriage, Mr. McLoughlin unexpectedly died of a heart attack, leaving Mrs. McLoughlin with four children at home to be raised in the upper-middle-income suburb in which they lived. Since that suburb was close to her own family and was noted for its excellent school system, Mrs. McLoughlin decided to keep the house and raise her children there.

Many times as a parent I have had experiences that were very important to me, but because of the age of the children or perhaps because it would have done more harm than good, I did not share these experiences with them. I don't think it is necessary for kids and parents to have to share everything with each other in order to be close. Maybe the kid who couldn't come to his parents and say, "I just took LSD," maybe it was wise for him to do that, because he can still remain close to his parents.

Ten or fifteen years ago, when the children were much younger of course, there was start of talk about drugs, about LSD—it became closer, it wasn't so abstract anymore. It was getting very close to home. Ten or fifteen years ago, I would have been shattered—completely destroyed at the idea that my children might have been smoking pot. I had the responsibility as both mother and father, and that would have meant to me that I was a failure. Ten years later, even now, if they tell me that they smoke pot—and they have—I'm not shocked anymore. What I am driving at is they, too, know that there is a right and a wrong time to share something or to talk to a parent about something and still be close. If they withhold some things, it is not because of a lack of confidence—it is because the timing may be wrong.

But I haven't evolved far enough yet in these ten years to let them smoke at home. Maybe five years from now I will feel differently about it. You see, I am still not sure about pot. I don't know whether it is good or it is bad. And I am not going to expose them in my home to something that just might not be good.

Things like pot smoking belong in a peer group. The same is true for sexual experiences. I think any parent that doesn't realize that there are going to be sexual experiences within the high school years is pretty much of an ostrich. But I don't think that my daughters have to come home to me and say, "Oh, I slept with John," or "Oh, I had an orgasm last night." I just don't think it is my business. If they are old enough to have the experience, they are old enough also to want the privacy of it. But if they are having a problem with it they could bring that to me. They can come to me for advice.

I always feel that a parent is a parent. I don't believe in this buddy-buddy—I am not my daughter's sister. Or girl friend. Or pal. Or peer. What I do want of her is to love me, to respect me, and to basically be friends with me. Again, you do share things with friends. However, there are very few friends—well, none that I've ever had that I've shared my husband's and my most intimate things with. I mean it is none of their business.

If my daughter came home with her boyfriend and wanted to sleep with him in her bedroom, I would not allow it. In my house, my daughter would sleep in her own room and the guest, be it male or female, would sleep in the guest room. When she is mistress of her home she can make certain rules and have certain things that she considers standards of her home. But in my home, I am the mistress.

If they can't make a few concessions to my rules, why should I make any to theirs? It's as simple as that. For instance, I go to visit my daughter who is in college. There are mixed dorms, and that is not shocking to me. These are the mores of this generation. I respect her school and her environment. I don't go down there to be shocked and to wave my hands, screaming about the boys; that's the way it is. And I would never embarrass her by making a big scene. I would expect the same treatment when she comes home, that she would respect my environment and my rules, and my way of life.

There is a natural evolution of living. Things change. Life changes. When I say that these are the rules of my house, all I'm saying is this is the way that I feel right now. I may change someday. Like my attitude toward pot has changed. I, myself, do not smoke pot. I have never done it. I don't think I need to. I don't think I want to. But then I don't drink to excess; and that doesn't mean in my mind that anyone who drinks to excess is necessarily a weirdo. Or an alcoholic. I guess it just has to do with tolerance. In the broad sense of the word. Not just tolerate or put up with. But to tolerate . . . as in to understand. If I can understand my kids and the way they want to live, then they should also be able to understand my rules and regulations.

Many young people today are living lives very different from their parents'. And many of these young people are right. Four years of college does not necessarily teach you how to live, and it doesn't really prepare you for very much today unless you are studying for a skilled profession, like medicine or law. If going to college is going in one door and coming out four years later, and it hasn't changed you at all, or hasn't taught you any-thing—then it's been a waste of time. A hypocrisy. I feel that college today is a holding tent for young people. And I think young people resent that, because that should be the real begin-ning of their productive years. And they are not being allowed to do anything productive. Now, as far as rejecting our economic affluence, I don't think they are rejecting it. I think they like the things that money buys. I think in the case of young people they think they have to make a choice. They have to give up the pursuit of money and embrace self-sacrifice because they think they are doing more for people that way. The sad thing is that they aren't. They are giving up comforts and a higher standard of living and really achieving nothing by doing it. The only way to lick the system is to get in there and be a part of it and work within it. I don't care what system it is.

It's been about ten years since the start of the Hippy Movement. And the system hasn't changed much in the ten years that some kids gave up affluence and wandered around in bare feet living in communes. Do you think that will ever really change anything? I agree with a lot of the thinking of young people. I agree with the reasons for the Youth Revolution. I really do. But I don't think that they are getting any place because I think in order to revolt, you not only have to have something to revolt against. The key is in having something that you are revolting toward.

So many young people who leave the United States waste themselves. I think that is very, very sad. Doing absolutely nothing. Whether it is in Afghanistan or here in the States. They are not contributing anything to society. And I know it is a cliché, but I think this is one of the goals of being a human being. They have a responsibility to contribute to society, to the living or the life of the people around them. Be it material, like something someone makes with their hands, or something he makes with his mind. But contributing something outside of himself.

Maybe if enough of those kids went to work for General Motors there would be change. People who now run General Motors won't live forever. And somewhere along the line, if those kids get in there, in ten years, instead of smoking pot and copping out and dropping out, a helluva lot of the top would fly off. Or fall off. And eventually you must replace it. I know many kids see the problem as getting rid of General Motors, not reforming it, and perhaps their ideals are right. I wish I could offer a solution for doing it. I don't have one. But I don't think the kids have one either.

I had a lot more hope ten or even five years ago for the young people, but not now. I felt that they were doing something then and that they might make it. I feel now that they've lost their way. I think there is a revolution going on; I just think it is not directed properly. Again, I'll go back to what I said before, a revolution should not only have certain goals to be destroyed —it should have goals and the means of rebuilding.

I, for one, have more faith in our young people than most

people. I think they are going to make the changes they want. They're going to do it. And they are going to do their own thing, too. Live their own lives. And eventually they will contribute to society—not just cop-out. They do come back. They will drift back. I think a lot of young people are. They're taking jobs and making their political views heard—not by yelling in the streets but by running for office. And I really think that is the only way they are going to do it.

I would like to see my son run for office. I'm very pleased that my daughter is so interested in politics, not because politics is the answer, but because it is one phase of a big, big problem. It shows that they are thinking, that they are interested enough to do something. Do something. Try. If enough of them did it, we would have the change that so many of them speak about. For example, why the hell didn't more kids vote in the last election?

The biggest gap between young people and people of my generation and the generation before me is the hypocrisy. It's a situation of, "Do what I say—but don't do as I do." You can't live that way. Kids are smart. Too smart. You can't say to a kid: "Be in by eleven o'clock." And then breeze in yourself, drunk, at four. Kids see this behavior. And sooner or later they imitate it.

There is a tremendous hypocrisy. As kids are growing up, and we are growing older, we don't like to admit to certain things. Certain mistakes. So, we cover. We rationalize. We lie about things. They see this very clearly, and that's not good. But it is not done with an evil intention—to hurt the kids. It's the other way around.

We do it as a protective measure. We want to protect ourselves, our own image. So we lie that way, too. Another hypocrisy. I think the middle-Europeans and the Latins have a much more realistic way of bringing up their children. In this country, if Mommy and Daddy have a fight, they go into the bedroom and shut the door and argue. If Poppa cheats, then Momma doesn't share that with anyone. So the kid grows up believing that this is a boy meets girl, boy dates girl, boy marries girl, live happily-ever-after world. In other words, not realistic.

As opposed to Europe, where everybody screams and gets it off their chest. Kids growing up in that kind of atmosphere have a more realistic picture of what life is really all about. There is a more real, down-to-earth, not so brittle atmosphere in the family. They scream. They love each other. They react to things visibly. And a little kid growing up sees this.

Before there is communication between parent and child, there has to be communication between father and mother. And so often there isn't any. Life today is very demanding for both parents. It's no picnic. And our young people are running away from it.

I don't understand why it is necessary to give up certain things and give up certain values in order to have a communication. I don't understand how it is possible to change the social structure. Don't these young people know, even in the countries they are in now, like Pakistan, that they are still in a different class? They are merely becoming the upper class of another society. They have an upward mobility.

That's not so far away from the mental and emotional thing that makes us drive for an upward mobility in the society that we are in. If these kids had to live in Afghanistan or India, or wherever, without those American dollars, at the same level that those natives are living at, and in the same situations, I don't know what they'd do. Some would stay, but not many. The fact is, what we need from the young people is understanding as to why father is doing some of the things that he is doing.

Look, people came to this country in search of something. They came with borrowed money. No knowledge of the language. Very little education. Most of the emigrants who came were illiterate. And they had to work. They gave their kids the most important thing that they could give them: an education. Education was the most wonderful thing they could give them. Both parents worked. Worked hard. Had shops. For what? To send their kids to school. To become Americans.

And what happened? They became so Americanized that

they were ashamed of their parents. I've seen this very often with first-generation Americans who now have an education and are ashamed of Momma and Poppa. Yet these are the people who worked and slaved for them, who sent them to school. Now the first-generation American becomes very interested in upward mobility. And he wants his kids to have it even better.

Now our own kids say they don't want this. They want no part of it. Maybe it had to stop. But our children should understand us. It wasn't so much that we were selfish or that we were only interested in material things; it was an effort to prove to these people—our parents and grandparents—that we could do it. It became achievement, plain and simple. If our kids could understand that, then maybe they wouldn't be so down on it. Do you see what I am driving at? These kids accuse us of a materialism that may not be the reason for what we are doing.

Our young people don't have to want what we wanted, but they can still respect us and what made us the way that we are. The exact same way that we should respect them and the way that they are. And the things they want. We went through a whole cycle. If this happened, it was Momma's fault. If that happened, it was Poppa's fault. I don't believe that! Parents were made to feel terribly guilty about everything. I don't think we should have been made to feel that way. You do the best you can under the circumstances, and if it doesn't turn out right, you don't crucify yourself. And so many kids seem to think that parents should crucify themselves for the mistakes they made. Yes, there are mistakes; we made them; they were honest mistakes. Our beliefs were honest beliefs. They are our beliefs. And as such they should be respected.

I respect my children's points of view, too, but I don't have to live their way. And I don't have to say that they should live mine. My prime role as a parent is to raise my children, give them a healthy body, give them a healthy, open, well-educated mind. By well-educated, I mean one that is receptive to experiences, all life experiences, to thought that is completely open, that can absorb as much as that mind can possibly take. But the ultimate role of the parent is to raise their children to be truly independent people who are capable of adjusting to whatever life brings to them. If I have done that one thing, then I have succeeded as a parent.

By giving children their freedom . . . that is really the best way of loving your children and thus keeping your children. But parents attempt other ways. They tie them by bonds of guilt, bonds of dependency.

History is repeating itself, too. I think there have been cycles in the history of man where young people have done exactly what they are doing now. Don't you think the immigration in the 1890's was in some respects a revolt of the young people against the standard of living, the way they lived in Europe? I don't think what today's children are doing is anything new or unique. I just think it is another way of expressing the same thing. Disgust with society. History has had many cases of young people leaving their homes in search of something else. And that is what we have now, I think. I just think what they are going *toward* is different. In their own minds, they really don't have a goal. To live their own lives? It's not enough. Nope. Do you know what I really can't understand? These kids, most of them are in their twenties, right? Well, what will they be like at thirty or forty? I don't think they know. Instant gratification. Me, me, me. Sounds very hedonistic. Well, it just ain't gonna work.

Maturity brings forth the ability to see or plan ahead. To go beyond the present moment. You can't get away from certain natural things, such as a woman's desire to have a child. To fulfill her biological function. It may sound ridiculous, but it isn't. And you will find that these young girls when they get into their forties suddenly find themselves going through meno-pause. And we'll have mental cases all over the place, because they have never had a child—and now they never will.

I don't think you can get away from the human satisfactions that have evolved through centuries of time. The girls wind up manifesting some of the things that they are now denying. You set up a commune and soon the nesting instinct comes out. Put up a curtain. A bunch of flowers. It's an instinct, as natural as breathing, as having your monthly period. And it's just as natural for the boy to be the hunter, the provider. You can do an awful lot about equalizing people, but there are some things you just can't change. The roles that people play are fine, as long as they don't deny the basic human role. Establishing the nucleus, the root, this is also part of the human condition. You need it. I'm frightened about what is going to happen to our young people. But I still have faith in them.

I feel that I have a very good rapport with young people, but I am unhappy at certain attitudes they have toward their parents, toward schools. They shrug their shoulders. They walk away. They are so quick to judge. Even to despair. They turn off. They tune you out. One important thing is confidence. An exchange of ideas. If young people want to be listened to, they should also want to listen. If they want to have their mores and their philosophies respected, they shouldn't abuse mine. I have as much right to my ideologies as they have to theirs. But young people do not listen. They do not want to hear.

I think it is a clear symptom of the way that a lot of young people were brought up. They never had to respect a parent's ideas. And many young people have lacked something because the parents were too busy. Discipline is good. It makes you able to live within yourself. Teaches you the boundaries of life. If we rebelled, we at least knew what we were rebelling against.

We had a very definite framework to work within. To live with. Some people have been given a great deal of freedom. Self-expression. Whatever they want. I call it lack of discipline. After all, this rebellion is necessary for growing up. It is part of the independence of the human spirit. I call it the cuttlebone. The little bird has to have the cuttlebone to scratch its beak against. And that can be supplied to a young person through discipline. If the parent cops out, then that's just as wrong. You can't be too dogmatic and you can't be too permissive. Everything must be in its time. Everything in its place. To tell you the truth, twenty years from now I'll tell you whether or not I've been successful. Right now I have six children and I think they are marvelous. I think they are truly great human beings. My best recommendation is my children themselves; they are my recommendation. Successful or not, they will prove me. Not what I say, but how they turn out. It will not be a question of *my* standards; it will be a question of *their* standards. How well they adjust . . . no matter where the world takes them. If they are able to act and to respond to those experiences, and to find their own measure of success or happiness, then that is the success. Not to be a lawyer or a doctor or make a million dollars. Not that kind of success. I just say: "Be happy in your own way." But being happy, that isn't the end-all or the be-all of existence either. You also have to give something back to the world. And be a part of the world. Not turn your back on it. Just find your own way to do it. I found mine. Now it's their turn. It doesn't matter what it is. But you've got to feel that you've done something. I can't tell them where to go or what to find. It's up to them. But whatever it is, or wherever they go, I'll respect them. All we can give them is understanding and love. Maybe direct them a little tiny bit—but not much.

Ultimately, they will have to find their own way. Their own direction. Their own happiness. And I've got to continue to find mine. I'm not dead yet. It's simple: until the day you die you grow. Until the day you die you have to keep living. All I can say is that I'm hopeful. I am. I really am.

"Be a part of the world. I found mine. Now it's their turn."

21 Kathryn and Matt

MATT: "Everyone is a beggar, you are yourself. A beggar in life. You are walking there, hoping you'll get something out of life."

KATHRYN: "Endurance is very important for young people."

A hot winding road and a red cloud of dust. The laughing sounds of children and a musical sound, like windchimes. As the dust settled, two barefooted strangers appeared. Her legs had many ankle bracelets and rings adorned her toes. Colored skirts danced around her ankles. She wore a gauzy peasant blouse, an enormous embroidered shawl, and tens of Persian and Indian Koochi necklaces. His feet were lean and caloused. He wore baggy white pants, a brightly colored Afghani farmer shirt, more necklaces, and the tail of a striped silk turban. They both had blazing blond hair and their bright blue eyes smiled at us.
Matt and Kathryn were walking into Kabul.

MATT: We came from India. We have been in Asia for
seven months now. And we are returning to India after our stay
in Afghanistan. But here we've been traveling around; not only
staying in Kabul. We are with a group of five people. Friends
whom we have met on the road. And we all made a pilgrimage
there together. And since then, we've been ripped off. Money
and passports.

KATHRYN: And Kabul is the worst place for that to happen. So we've been waiting an x amount of time here. And in
that amount of time the revolution has happened, so we've been
really held down in Kabul.

MATT: It's a different group here of young people than
there is in Goa, for instance, or Katmandu. You know, some
people come this far east and stop at Kabul. Then they turn
around and go back from here.

KATHRYN: It's like a trip for the summer and then going
back. But if our parents were to see us now, they would go, *Oh
my God!*

MATT: My father is dead now, and I haven't seen my
mother in many years. I'm sure she has gone through changes,
too. If she hasn't turned on, I would offer her the chance to
smoke or to take any hallucinogen or drug that I might have on
me. Then perhaps we could understand each other a little better.
I don't know whether she would be loose enough to do that.
That's what one wonders, you know. One always hopes that
contact will be made. With your parents, it's often a dream. I
think it would be a very great compliment to your parents to
have their child score them some dope before they die.

KATHRYN: My parents would never turn on. First of all, I
would never suggest it. They are not even drinkers. And they
are very much upstanding American citizens . . . raise the flag in

the backyard every day. They are New England people, from Sweden.

MATT: When I grew up it was the usual middle-class American thing. My father was in importing and exporting. Shipping. He was Catholic so I was raised a Catholic. Roman Catholic. And I went to a Jesuit School. There were problems at the time. Oh, I think seventh grade was the hardest. There was always a big scene with my parents, because one started to smoke and drink at a very early age. Beer and cigarettes at the age of nine. And I was really into bourbon at the age of thirteen. Completely drunk, that was part of it. To be a high school kid. To be running around in a car. To be drunk on the beach. My parents turned away. They didn't want to know. They knew if they knew, they would be upset.

KATHRYN: Exactly. Right.

MATT: They didn't want to know. As long as the graduating class had no girl pregnant, you know. That's all they wanted to know. And in the meantime, if there were blue movies . . . okay. So innocent because we were provincial Americans, too.

KATHRYN: That was like us. We were four children. All very different. And treating each one alike, you know. And never really talking. There was a wall up about what they believed in. You couldn't penetrate that. There was no arguing. There was no understanding at all. That wall was just there. That was it. So I jumped over the wall . . . or climbed out the window.

I had a lot of pressure in high school to go to college. So I went and studied political science. I was a cheerleader in high school. Very rah, rah. All-American. I loved it at the time. I had a fantastic time. All that energy on the football field. The color. The action. Then I went to college. I was studying political science in Washington, D.C., at the same time that I was working on Capital Hill for Bobby Kennedy. Then I went on his campaign with him. I was standing in the kitchen with him when he was killed. And that really ended all my political dreams, which really centered around him anyway, I guess. That whole Kennedy background was much stronger than I had thought, coming from New England and all. But after being in Washington, I became completely disillusioned. I learned that the system wasn't really worth it after all. You see I learned how it all really works. Well, by the time McGovern was running, I had left the political arena and I was traveling abroad.

I went to Paris. I was glad to leave college. The curriculum, grading, very, very bad. Bad teaching. Bad examinations. Each teacher has his own phobia. His own way of examining. You were the victim.

In college I smoked grass. I was going to school, I was working all day long while I was going to school. But I liked the atmosphere . . . At that time, people were all involved in protests and a lot of different things and I liked that. There was a great feeling of hope in those days. I don't feel that way now.

MATT: I left America thirteen years ago. Yes. And I haven't been back since. I left with my parents and we went to Australia. My father had business there and he just dreamed of going to Australia before he died. And so we went. And I started school there . . . in the system; but I couldn't take it, so I stopped almost immediately. I never went back. I went to art school instead. Started working on a newspaper. After that, I left Australia and came to Europe where I lived.

I went to western Europe. Parts of eastern Europe, too. Austria. Yugoslavia. Greece . . . I went that way. Spent many years in London, Paris, Spain, Morroco. Yes, I have an American passport. But I never really experienced all that transition that happens during the teens in America on American soil. But the formative years of my life were spent in America. American morals. And American mores. The American way. I feel American. I am an American. I was raised as an American. My parents were both American, and their parents were born in

America. And I'm one of the first to leave. My sister still lives in America.

I'm the only one who left the family. Just started out on my own. I haven't seen them since then. I've kept in touch . . . writing them letters. But one day I received a letter from my mother that was just so embarrassing that it was unreal. I didn't really know who she was anymore. I had written her a very enthusiastic letter telling her who I was and where I was and trying to deal with the life that I was leading. Then she sent me a news clipping. She had given my letter to the paper for their social section. So here is this clipping about me being in Morocco. If that's where she is at, then I don't need to write to her anymore. And I haven't written her since.

I was very angry. Something very personal. I wrote her a letter and the letter was reprinted in the newspaper. She's an American social matron. She works for charity. She does things like that. Outside of the social register, the Sunday newspaper in America is an important status thing. Photographs and names mentioned. Everything spelled correctly. It's an important aspect—that's the American Dream. The snobbery. All the status. All the labels. It's all just been put into you from television and mass media from when you are so young. When you really know all that aspect of American life, that's when you are really an American. The amount of times you have been to a drive-in, the amount of times you have had TV dinners, the amount of times you have been to the country club. For some people it's not the kind of thing you want to get away from.

As a child, my fancy turned in different ways. Like Stevenson. Or Marilyn Monroe. Everything else was grey. My childhood: going to school—there were very few things to attach on to. Later on, when reading American History, you see things more clearly. But when you are in the middle of it as a child, there are strange refuges you take. And one of them was certainly Hollywood.

At the same time, we certainly appreciate our upbringing a little bit more. We didn't know what it was before. Because you are human. You want to cry about the pain you see throughout the world. You don't know what to do. The heat, the women, the children, and everyone . . . with just no money, you know. It's an inferno. What can you do in the face of that? Everyone is a beggar; you are yourself. A beggar in life. You are walking there, hoping you'll get something out of life.

KATHRYN: But there's another aspect of it, too. People call this an underdeveloped world. Well, what about calling America the overdeveloped world? I spent a few years in Europe and, for me, it was a great awakening after having been in the States. My eye changed entirely. In my childhood, underneath, there were a lot of values that I believed in. I agreed with them. But now it's from a different angle.

For example, art can be political. And men can live in many different ways. We're political now. Young people are a minority and we should have rights. And we don't. So we get screwed all over the world.

But we just continue. Endurance is very important for young people. For everybody right now . . . to endure. You see people of different ages and you see somebody twenty-eight or thirty and they've gone through so many different changes; they are over the hump. You see something else than you see in a nineteen-year-old. I think endurance is very, very important.

MATT: We've been traveling with one another for two years and we see our future as pretty much together. We also have many friends around the world. We visit each other, and run into each other. We are all into drugs, too—drugs keep me living. It's like a rendezvous . . . that next time when you are going to take a hallucinogen. You've gone through a specific time with it and when you take that drug you go back to that time with it. It's like a link with that drug and that experience. It opened up a whole new world for me . . . LSD. Well, it's the impermanence of that phenomenon. I was made conscious of the transience of all things. First of all, perhaps most importantly of all, the loss of ego. The moment of truth. The world. The colors. Verbs. Positive things. But drugs are not for everyone.

I'm a fascist about that. I've seen the bad results of drug-taking, too. Like with heroin-users, it's no longer your emotions. You don't want to feel because you can't handle it. The negative thing becomes the force behind the drug-taking, instead of just an experiment. I should know—I've had about five hundred or more trips on acid. One of the main things about taking drugs is to be out in nature. Afghanistan is perfect in that respect. It's one of the great pleasures left in the world.

KATHRYN: I feel the same way that he does . . . that it's a positive thing for me. I feel very good about drugs because I've only had good experiences. I feel that I had been as conventional as possible because of my background. I had a very hard time holding back. And I did, for a long, long time. Finally, when I left the country, and I was on my own, drugs became part of my family.

MATT: It comes about through some sort of mutual recognition. Some of my best friends I have met just flashing at them on the streets. We were total strangers. We didn't know each other's names. But we certainly knew each other's ethics when we approached one another. And for that reason we became friends—seemingly out of nowhere. At a cafe or some place public. And after that, a very intimate relationship evolves. If we are not together, we exchange letters or telephone calls or words through other people. These friends have become our family. You get from these friends things that you didn't get from your family. Very few words are necessary. It's not necessary to speak to be demonstrative. Great periods of reading, too. The classics. Philosophers . . . Nietzsche . . . Dostoevsky . . . Cocteau . . . Ronald Firbank . . . Genêt. Those people have really opened the world for us, have created an atmosphere. Those writers are part of our group.

KATHRYN: I don't think of myself as part of a group. In Asia here, true, there is a group, because they run all the good places. And so you gotta go. You want to see those places.

MATT: We have friends in Nepal who produce books and photography and publish poetry. Another friend of mine is writing a book on correspondences. Another friend is a poet. Another is writing a book on the dope scene. These are the sorts of things that are being produced. At the moment, I am just traveling. It's a great feeling of freedom to come to Asia. Especially after the restrictions of the West. You can step free here. You can wear what you want. You can take as many drugs as you want, appear how you want in public. You don't have to worry; there is no paranoia. In the States, it was very hard to move freely. One had friends with whom you smoked or went with to a club at night. There are all these little centers in the West, but you mostly stayed in the pad. Whereas here, it's all outdoors.

KATHRYN: You know, we didn't come out here to explain why we are here. We're just out here. You know, there is a great sense of anything can happen.

MATT: The spiritual quest is very tiring. And it's a great cliché. It is exhausting and I've seen it in many faces. And I've felt it myself when I had a brush with Buddhism. It got awfully heavy. It takes the center away from your life, as it is here. You know, right here and now. And it puts it out somewhere else —somewhere metaphysical. In the end, it was one big physical sensation that you were attracted to. . . . Swimming in the lake in the Arabian Sea. Staying in Goa on the beach. For two months we lived without any structure whatsoever. We just lived on the beach and slept in the sand. We didn't even make a little palm hut; we just slept right on the beach itself. The conditions were ideal—it was that kind of a situation. It made one feel that life somehow was bigger again. There weren't any more confinements. They were only there if you put them there.

My day always depends on where I am. Our day, for instance, here in Kabul, we are in a big town, so our day is very much like anyone's day in a big town. You are under the same influences. You are exposed to the same things that everyone is exposed to. Everyone gets very confused at the bazaar. So you have to cool it.

Some days we stay home. We have a garden and we share a house with some people. Some English people. And we sit in the garden and we make tea and we smoke hash and we read and we draw and we write letters and we talk a lot and we cook food and we wash our clothes and life is very simple. I suppose it could be considered selfish. Or perhaps just natural.

KATHRYN: Sometimes we think of having kids. Eventually. When I can manage it, you know. But we won't marry in the formalistic sense of the word. I have a great abhorrence for paperwork.

I've seen marriage. My God, I've seen it. I went to a public high school in the States. And, like, all those people are married now. And many, many of them are also divorced now. And they don't know what to do with themselves. They just lock into whatever situation they happen to be in. There's no vision whatsoever.

I've seen some great successes with girls who've had babies. But I've also seen some flipped-out girls who have given their babies in their arms LSD. Some very strange situations in India where the child has almost died through neglect because the mother had no natural feelings. I've seen two examples of that where the baby was almost dead. But it was all part of a scene. Somebody comes in and sees the kid and takes it up and then takes care of it for two months and then the baby is okay. So everyone looks after each other, especially as far as the children are concerned. They have a fantastic life. When I see the nine-year-old and ten-year-old kids on the head scene, on the moving scene, like wow! They can take care of themselves.

I think people should be a good example to children, because they copy everything you do.

MATT: Children can do many things. In fact, they live out all the lives that you don't. Children are us. At what point, at what age, are you supposed to grow up? That's a great American myth. Twenty-one or eighteen? Or sixteen? A date or a time. That isn't how it is at all. Some mutation or something different happens at a different age. It's not necessarily when they dictate it.

The future is fascinating because the future also contains one's death. And that's the one rendezvous you've got in life for sure. And in the meantime all the moments of spontaneity, and all of the moments of rejoicing are the things one looks forward to.

Soon we are going to South India at Christmas time. America likes to be happy at Christmas. But personal happiness isn't so important. It only comes . . . three minutes, five minutes, ten minutes, you know. But generally to acquire peace, that's the important thing. One's happiness—it's like a birthday party. You want to cry in the end. It's very wonderful when it comes; but then it goes. If parents understood that truth, they wouldn't be so possessive about their kids. Lack of possessiveness is terribly important. And also the idea that it's to their own child's advantage that the child leave home as soon as possible. It's the trauma in America with mothers and fathers and children.

I don't know what happens between parents and children. Some great mystique. We have friends in Europe who have five children and they are incredible parents because they are able to leave their children. They have continued with their lives. So many children are kept babies by their parents.

KATHRYN: Americans particularly make babies out of their children. They talk down to their child. A lot of fathers want their sons to be what they weren't. They want their sons to be, to be, to be. That was the pressure in my family. You had to excel and you had to be the best. All of these things going on create a lot of tension in the home and outside of the home and in the playgrounds.

MATT: But you can't make any rules. There isn't any set age when the child should leave home. It's like Kazan, the film director, who said it's up to your own intelligence as to when you escape. It's no good referring back to a younger brother, saying I am going back and kidnap him, because they've got to get away from home. If people don't know where the escape door is, perhaps there isn't one in their life.

My mother was very possessive, and it was very hard to escape from her. I mean it was. I had run away from home. They had forced me into that. Running away. And I had to write to them for money . . . some place abroad. It was completely crazy and they turned me into a truant from life. It took a long time not to have the psychological relationship with them, just to be free of them. To be ready to meet them. My father died in the meantime. But I want to meet my mother again. On an equal level without all the anxiety of before.

I feel there is another step in my life, and I can use my experience to create. Because that's what we all want to do anyway. That's a very basic desire—to create outside yourself. But I'm not anticipating . . . or pushing. I know that I am going to write someday. I know it. I see it as another stratum. Nothing like my parents, no.

KATHRYN: I don't think I will end up like my parents in terms of life style. But I don't feel so much of a rebellion toward my parents, because there was a great amount of love despite the other confusing issues. I don't consider the way we live as a rebellion. I don't think of it in terms like that at all. I am in the process of growing. I grow in many different directions.

Kathryn and Matt are pioneers. They are pioneering their future lives.

Kathryn leaves behind her family and a dead Kennedy. Matt leaves behind his mother and America. But they are American and they know it.

Their future is inextricably bound to the East. If they ever return, listen to them, for Matt has hope, and Kathryn has endurance.

22 Mrs. Palmer

"I have absolutely nothing to say."

We finally reached Mrs. Palmer by telephone. She lives in a fashionable northern California suburb. We had to contact her through her personal secretary. We had hoped to set up an interview with her.

Matt? I have absolutely nothing to say about him. I did receive a letter from my eldest son. He deigned to write. It was the first time we'd heard from him in years. He said he didn't feel bitter about us anymore. He wanted to open channels of communication. To see how we all were. To share his life experiences. "How is father?" he asked. Father had died the year before. There had been no way to notify his son. My daughter is married now. The children are gone or grown. What does he expect of us? To welcome home the prodigal?

I have nothing to say about him. He's gone. Far away. Dead.

force people into a drug subculture which fosters disrespect for the law and creates a context for experimentation with more dangerous ''hard'' drugs. Just as Prohibition did not stop Americans from drinking alcohol, so the present laws are ineffective in stopping the smoking of marijuana. Marijuana, like alcohol, is here to stay and we'd better start figuring out ways to control consumption.

In addition, we saw that young people need new frontiers. That is why, in a psychological sense, the Westward Movement was so important to Americans. There was a place to pioneer and test one's skills of survival. We need to create new frontiers for our people.

Finally, we believe that social institutions are not abstractions, if only because their effects on our personal and family lives are self-evident. When we allow the American Medical Association to artificially control the number of doctors by restricting the number of admissions to medical school, it may be your child who is not admitted. When we allow impoundment of federal funds for education, it may be your child who is forced to leave college because there is no financial aid for him. And when we allow our government to commit war crimes in Vietnam, we scar an entire generation.

In the course of our travels, we visited a Maine family that supported itself by lobster fishing. The eleven-year-old son directly contributed to the support of his family by selling the lobsters he caught in his traps. He had to go out in his boat every day to check his traps. He had built the boat himself with the help of his father and grandfather. He had also built the traps himself. He knew how far he could safely take his boat out because his father told him the limits. When he returned, he often would have one of the traps with him because he needed to repair it.

This young person had a tremendous sense of himself. His contribution to his family was palpably real. He knew what skills he had. He was disciplined and responsible. His feeling of self-identity was evident in his self-assurance. It is unlikely, we think, that he will become an exile.